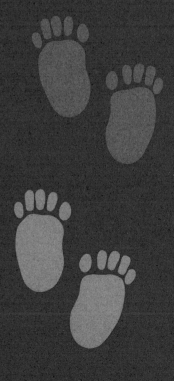

Making Lovable
Teddy Bears &
Their Clothes

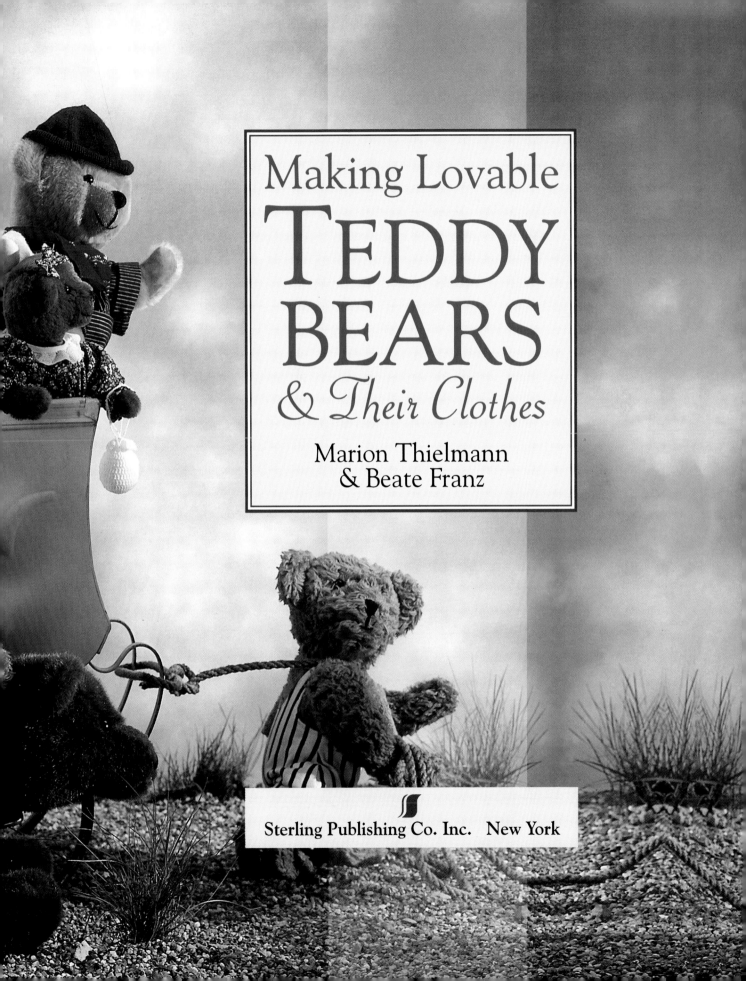

Making Lovable
TEDDY
BEARS
& Their Clothes

Marion Thielmann
& Beate Franz

Sterling Publishing Co. Inc.   New York

The written instructions, photographs, designs, patterns, and projects in this volume are intended for the personal use of the reader and may be reproduced for that purpose only. Any other use, especially commercial use, is forbidden under law without the written permission of the copyright holder.

Every effort has been made to ensure that all the information in this book is accurate. However, due to differing conditions, tools, and individual skills, the publisher cannot be responsible for any injuries, losses, and other damages which may result from the use of the information in this book.

The authors and their bears are as follows:* **Marion Thielmann:** Oscar (Oskar), Herbert, Benny and Christopher (Christoph), Goldie (Zotty), Henrietta (Henriette), and Brownie (Brauni). The text for the chapter on basic techniques is also by Marion Thielmann. **Beate Franz:** Bartleby (Bärtl), Pete (Fiete), Ralph (Ralf), Pearl (Puschel), Scotty, Lisa, and Brownie (Brauni).

*Some bears have been renamed for the English edition, in which case their original German names are given in parentheses above.

Photography: Roland Krieg, Waldkirch; drawings: Traudl Marks-Collet, Idstein
Patterns: Peter Beckhaus, Mainz, from designs by the authors.
English translation by Elizabeth Reinersmann; English translation edited by Isabel Stein. Thanks to Ron and Elke Block of Edinburgh Imports, Inc., Newbury Park, California, for help with the English edition the book.

Library of Congress Cataloging-in-Publication Data
Thielmann, Marion.
[Teddys, Nähanleitungen für Teddybären und ihre Kleidung. English]
   Making lovable teddy bears & their clothes / Marion Thielmann and Beate Franz.
      p. cm.
   Includes index.
   ISBN 0-8069-9712-5
   1. Soft toy making.   2. Teddy bears.   3. Doll clothes—Patterns.
   I. Franz, Beate.   II. Title. III.   Title: Making lovable teddy bears and their clothes.
TT174.3.T4813 1997
745.592′4—dc21   96-49193
                                                                          CIP

10 9 8 7 6 5 4 3 2 1

First paperback edition published in 1998 by
Sterling Publishing Company, Inc.
387 Park Avenue South, New York, N.Y. 10016
Originally published in Germany under the title
Teddys: Nähanleitungen für Teddybären und ihre Kleidung
© 1996 by FALKEN Verlag GmbH, Neidernhausen/Ts.,
 Germany
English translation © 1997 by Sterling Publishing Company, Inc.
Distributed in Canada by Sterling Publishing
% Canadian Manda Group, One Atlantic Avenue, Suite 105
Toronto, Ontario, Canada M6K 3E7
Distributed in Great Britain and Europe by Cassell PLC
Wellington House, 125 Strand, London WC2R 0BB, England
Distributed in Australia by Capricorn Link (Australia) Pty Ltd.
P.O. Box 6651, Baulkham Hills, Business Centre,
NSW 2153, Australia
Printed in Hong Kong
All rights reserved

Sterling ISBN 0-8069-9712-5 Trade
              0-8069-9713-3 Paper

CONTENTS

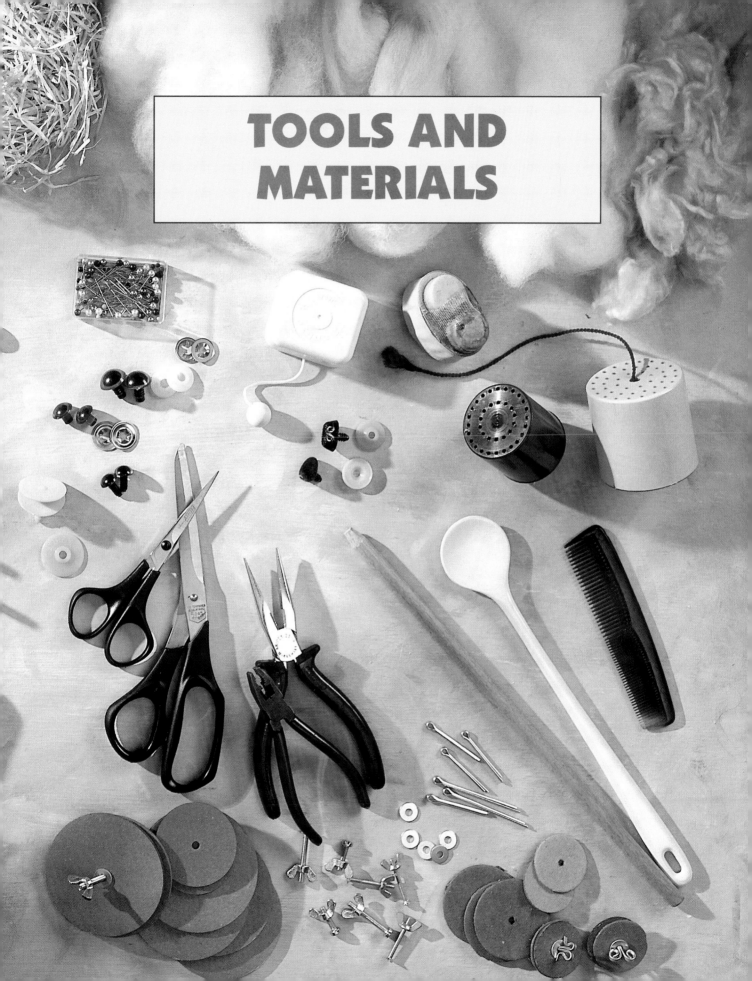

TOOLS AND MATERIALS

TOOLS & MATERIALS

Tools

It is likely that you already have some of the tools you will need. The rest can easily be found in hobby shops, fabric stores, doll and teddy bear supply stores, and mail-order catalogs. You will need:

- strong scissors for cutting paper
- sharp, pointed sewing scissors
- tracing paper
- medium heavy cardboard (like oaktag or a manila folder)
- craft glue or hot glue gun
- marking tools
  - permanent very fine pointed felt-tipped pen for dark fabrics
  - chalk or fabric marking pencil for light-colored fabrics and velvet (the marks will fade over time)
- straight pins with plastic heads such as quilting pins
- embroidery and darning needles
- thimble
- 4 inch to 5½ inch long (10 to 14 cm) needle for attaching glass eyes
- flat-nosed and needlenosed pliers
- stick or wooden spoon to use when stuffing
- awl for making joint holes in fur
- sewing machine (but everything can be sewn by hand, using doubled thread or buttonhole thread)
- thread
  - polyester thread for the seams
  - basting thread
  - strong thread for attaching the eyes (e.g., leather, or the cotton yarn used for crocheting doilies)
- thin black or brown woolen yarn, pearl cotton, or embroidery thread to embroider noses and mouths.

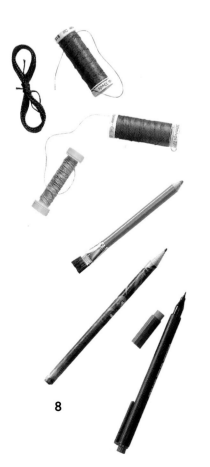

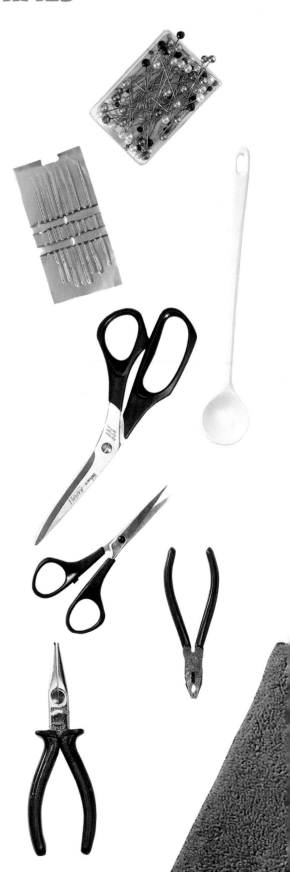

Fabrics for the Bears' Fur

General Comments

We have used many different fabrics for the bears in this book. The fabrics used are only suggestions; any bear can be made from the material of your choice. But please note that long-haired fur fabric is not suitable for the smaller bears.

Fur

Fur fabrics can be found in fabric stores, hobby shops, and by mail order from companies that sell teddy bear products. You may also use tightly woven, thick woolen coat fabric (camel hair), velvet, velour, and many other fabrics.

Fur fabrics are usually available in 54 or 60 inch (1.4 or 1.6 meter) widths. There are two basic kinds of fur fabrics: those with woven bases and those that are knitted.

Woven Fur Fabrics

Woven fur fabrics have a woven base that is firm. It will keep its shape when stuffed. Synthetic and mohair plush fabrics with woven bases usually are high-quality fabrics and easy to handle. For some time now, manufacturers have offered synthetic nonflammable fabric of polyacryl and modacryl fibers, which is washable and thus a very good choice for a bear made for a small child.

Knitted Fur Fabrics

Knitted fur fabrics have a knitted back side and are more or less stretchable. These materials are for the most part made from synthetic fibers or cotton. Some of these fabrics are washable (check washing instructions) and are an inexpensive alternative to the fabrics described above.

Materials for Paws and Soles

For the paws and soles of the feet you may use velvet, tightly woven wool or cotton fabric, soft leather, imitation suede, felt, or the wrong side of a fur fabric in a contrasting or

REMINDER
Stretchy fabrics should be reinforced on the back with iron-on interfacing (or with an extra layer of plain cotton). This will prevent the fabric from bagging or tearing during sewing, which would cause the bear to lose its shape.

Tip: When shopping for fabric, pay attention to the quality of the materials. High-quality fabric will not only extend the life of your teddy bear, but also your enjoyment of it.

Fur fabrics. From left to right: 1, 2: Knitted, cotton base. 3: Looped pile, woven base. 4, 5: Synthetic fur, woven base. 6: Wool, woven base. 7–11: Mohair, woven base.

complementary color to your bear's body. If you do not want to emphasize the paws and soles, cut them from the same material as the body, turned wrong-side out. If you don't want to emphasize the paws, combine the paw and inner arm patterns and cut them from a single piece of material, instead of cutting them separately. If you are using the fabric right-side out, you may want to trim the fur close to the base fabric with a sharp-pointed pair of scissors (see Photo 34) on the paws and soles. If

you want to use felt or another stretchable fabric for the paws, you can reinforce it with iron-on interfacing. Since synthetic felt wears out rather easily, it is not a good choice for bears made for small children; however, wool felt is more durable.

Velvet fabric ravels easily; it is therefore best to zigzag stitch each piece all the way around the edges (staystitch) before you start construction, or use milliner's glue. Staystitch very close to the cut edge.

From left to right: 1–4, felt; 5–7, velvet; 8–10, leather.

Eyes

Eyes for teddy bears come in many different forms, colors, and sizes. Glass eyes have a wire loop in the back and are attached after the head has been stuffed, sewn on with strong thread (see photos 31 and 32). The reflecting glass surface of the

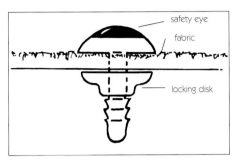

eyes gives teddy bears a very lifelike expression.

    Teddy bears for small children should have plastic safety eyes that come with a childproof snap-on attachment system (see drawing). Attach safety eyes to the fabric before stuffing the head (see pp. 21 and 22).

Nose and Mouth

Embroider the nose and mouth with brown or black woolen yarn, pearl cotton, or embroidery thread. Or use a plastic, glass, or velvet nose. There are childproof plastic noses that attach like the childproof plastic eyes; attach before stuffing the head.

Tip: When buying eyes, check that the pupils are both the same size.

NOTE
Noses made of velvet wear out quickly and become unsightly.

Joints

There are several different attachment systems for joining the head, arms, and legs to the body.

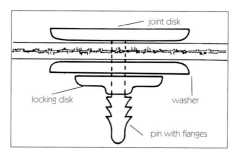

Plastic Joints

These are the parts you need:
- joint disks with snap-on pin (the pin has a set of flanges to catch the disk).
- washer
- locking disk

Plastic joints are light and easy to install. Since they are washable, they are excellent for teddy bears made for small children. You can't make fine adjustments on joints with a flange system, however.

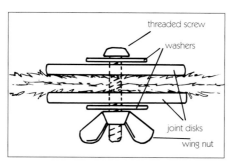

Screw Joints

For each joint you need:
- two joint disks with holes in the center, made of plywood, pressed cardboard, or plastic
- threaded screw
- wing-nut or locknut
- two washers

Screw joints are easy to install and can be fine-tuned.

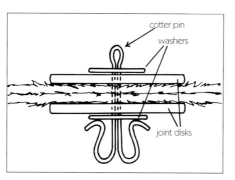

Cotter-Pin Joints

For each joint you need:
- two plywood or pressed cardboard joint disks with holes in the center
- one cotter pin
- two washers

The disks are connected by the cotter pin, whose ends are bent like a snail or a crown with a needlenosed pliers to secure it. It takes some practice to learn to do this. You can flatten the loop of the cotter pin to a T to keep it from pulling through the washer.

Tip: Smooth sharp edges of joint disks or cover them with felt to prevent the fabric in the area of the joint from wearing out prematurely.

Stuffing

In the past, teddy bears were usually stuffed with wood shavings (excelsior). This is still used for classical reproductions, although the process is a bit more complicated. Excelsior is lighter than other materials and can be obtained from teddy bear supply catalogs. To use it, roll small pieces into balls and stuff. A teddy bear stuffed with excelsior will lose its shape if it gets wet.

Washed sheep wool and high-quality polyester stuffing are very good. Synthetic fibers can be laundered in water as hot as 104°F (40°C); check the manufacturer's instructions for specifics. Synthetics do not clump up, they are hypoallergenic, and they remain odorless.

High-loft polyester stuffing is another synthetic stuffing. It works particularly well for those super-soft cuddly bears. Because this filling is very elastic, a teddy bear stuffed with it retains its shape, even if less stuffing is used.

Synthetic pellets should only be used for smaller bears. They are available in different sizes and are washable in temperatures up to 104°F (40°C); check the manufacturer's instructions. For larger bears, you may combine pellets with other stuffings. Pellets will not give much firmness to the body, but will leave the bear pliable and cuddly. Don't use pellets or anything small enough to be eaten in teddy bears for young children, or to stuff bear heads.

Kapok is a very fibrous natural material that is easy to work with. It goes a long way and is often the preferred material for larger bears. Bears

stuffed with kapok should not get wet, as it tends to clump.

The Voice Box (Growler)

You can choose among several different tones, depending on the size of bear you are making. These devices are placed in the body while the bear is being stuffed (see Photo 27).

Music Boxes

Teddy bears that have music boxes inside are particular favorites of babies and small children. Music boxes come with different melodies and can be found in hobby shops and from manufacturers of doll and teddy bear supplies. For more about how to insert them, see Photo 28.

From left to right: Excelsior (wood shavings), synthetic pellets, kapok, high-loft polyester stuffing, and washed sheep wool.

BASIC TECHNIQUES

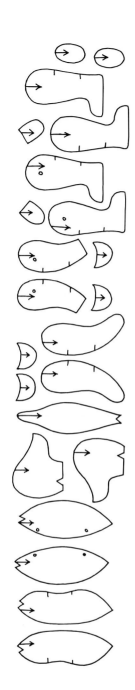

WORKING WITH PATTERNS

The pattern pieces are easy to copy and are given full size. Specific instructions are given with every pattern. The letters on the patterns help you know where pattern pieces are to be matched up. A key to the symbols and terms on the patterns is given on page 33. To fit in our book size, some pattern pieces for the larger bears and their clothes have been broken into parts (part 1, part 2, etc.). In that case, trace out the parts and join them at the joining lines as instructed before you make the pattern template or cut out the fabric.

The patterns may be enlarged or reduced. Just adjust the amount of fabric you buy and the size of the disks used for the joints. The diameter of a disk should be about ½ inch (1 cm) smaller than the diameter of the arm or leg in which it will fit. The disks used to attach the head to the body are usually a little larger than the ones for the limbs. They should fit exactly into the neck opening.

Making Templates and Preparing Fabrics

Since paper patterns tend to move when placed on fabric, make a cardboard template of each pattern piece:
- First, copy all pieces to tracing paper, including all markings and instructions. If a pattern piece is given in parts, join them along the joining lines to make one pattern piece.
- Glue the tracing paper to thin cardboard (the weight of a manila fold-

er) and cut out the templates.
- In order to avoid overlooking a pattern piece, complete all templates before cutting fabric.
- Fur fabric cannot be cut out when it is folded, because it is too thick. To cut a bear piece in which the pattern has a fold, trace the pattern onto *folded tracing paper* and cut out the pattern from the paper. Then open out the tracing paper to give you the whole pattern and make a template of the whole piece.
- If instructions say "cut 2 (1 R)," it means cut one with the pattern facing up and cut another with the pattern facing down (mirror image or reverse of the original pattern). Mark this on your template also.
- With a thick darning needle or an awl, poke holes at the dots in the templates where the joints are to be placed, so you can mark through on your fabric later.
- For a washable teddy bear, wash cotton fabrics before cutting fabric to avoid shrinkage later on.
- Reinforce very stretchy fabrics on the back with iron-on interfacing before cutting the pieces. Test on a scrap piece to see if the fabric will withstand the heat needed to fuse the interfacing. Let the fabric cool completely once fused.

Tracing to Fabric and Cutting
- Place the fabric face down on a flat work surface.
- Place the templates on the fabric, with enough room around them to

add seam allowances of ⅜ to ½ inch (0.75 to 1.0 cm). The large arrows on the pattern indicate the direction of the fabric's nap—the direction in which the fur lies on furry fabrics.

- The fur should lie down or diagonally down along the body and limbs. To find out which way the nap lies, move your hand over the surface, either parallel to or at 90° to the selvage of the fabric. Mark the direction of the nap with an arrow on the wrong side of your fur fabric. Align the long arrows on your pattern pieces parallel to the nap arrow on the fur fabric, when positioning.

- Before you cut, double check the pattern's instructions to see which pieces are to be cut twice or four times, and which are cut as a reverse (R).

- Trace around the templates with a thin permanent marker on the wrong side of the fabric (Photo 1). Transfer all information and symbols to fur. Leave room for seam allowances between the pieces.

- Cut out all pieces, adding the seam allowances as you cut (about ⅜ to ½ inch (0.75 to 1 cm); see Photo 2). Keep a standard width of seam allowance throughout; this will make sewing easier.

- When you cut the fabric, make sure that the pile of the fur is not cut, especially if the pile is very long. Cut the base of the fabric only, and do so in small steps. It is best to use a sharp pair of pointed scissors or a craft knife.

- Use a contrasting color of thread to make tacking stitches to mark where the joints and ears are to be placed (Photo 3).

1. Position the pattern on the fabric.

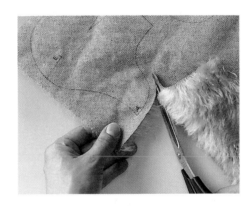

2. When cutting, make sure that the width of the seam allowance you add is the same for every piece.

3. Transfer the joint and ear attachment symbols from the back to the front of the fabric with thread.

4. Smooth the pile toward the inside and pin the pieces together.

5. Pull out the pile that has been caught in the seam with a needle.

6. Pieces are machine-basted together before sewing. Keep the pins in for this step.

7. Seam allowances of any curved areas are notched after sewing.

SEWING AND ASSEMBLY

- Read all the instructions in this chapter before starting a project. They are applicable for all teddy bears. Special situations are noted below or in the instructions for the particular project.
- Proceed with care and be accurate from the very beginning. You will see that the effort is well worth it.

Important Starting Tips

- Staystitch the stuffing openings of each part with large zigzag stitches to prevent the fabric from fraying later when the animal is stuffed. Do this first, before you start assembling the bear.
- Note that in some patterns the ears are sewn into the dart seam, so don't close those too soon.
- Organize the pieces of the pattern. The letters, numbers, and symbols help you know which get joined with which. Assemble with right sides of fabric facing each other, unless otherwise noted. Pin, baste, and then sew them together.
- To avoid catching the fur pile in the seams when sewing, move the pile in away from the edges before sewing (Photo 4). If some pile has been caught, use a needle or comb to free any from between the seam allowances and from the outside of the part after sewing (Photo 5).
- Fur fabric has a tendency to slide easily when the pieces are placed together. To keep this from happening, leave the pins in the fabric, perpendicular to the seam (Photo

6). With the longest possible stitch, machine-baste the pieces together with the pins still in place. This method replaces hand basting and allows short stretches to be undone without redoing all of the basting.

- After basting, double-check all symbols and lines to be sure they are lined up well.
- Next, stitch the final seam, using a setting that makes for a strong seam (for instance, a stretch stitch or a very narrow zigzag stitch) so that the seam will withstand the pressure of stuffing the animal. The final seam is stitched right over the basting stitches, which do not have to be removed.
- Fur fabric with a deep or long pile is more difficult to handle than fabric with a short pile. If your sewing machine can't sew through such thick fabric—which may happen when several layers have to be sewn together—sew them by hand. Use a thimble to help push the needle through thick layers.
- The seam allowances of curves and angles should be carefully notched after the seams have been sewn (Photo 7).
- After stuffing, turn in the seam allowances of the stuffing openings and hand-stitch them in place with strong thread.

Head and Ears

The head usually consists of two side pieces, a middle piece (head gusset), and four ear pieces (see diagram to the right). Sometimes the side piece is made of 2 separate pieces, as for Oscar. Sometimes the ears are inserted in the seam when the head is

Tools and materials of a well-stocked workshop.

REMINDER
All construction is done with right sides of fabric facing, unless noted.

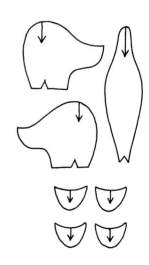

made; or you could sew them onto the completed head later by hand (see page 29).

- To assemble an ear, place an ear piece and its reversed piece, R, with right sides of fabric together and edges aligned, and sew them together along the curved outer edge. Notch the seam allowances for ease of turning (see Photo 7), and turn the ear right-side out.
- To make the ears firmer, add a little bit of stuffing inside.
- If you are inserting the ear into the head seam, close the ear opening with some basting stitches, without turning in the seam allowances, and baste the ears carefully in the correct place on the head pieces. They will be machine stitched in place when the dart or head seam is closed.
- Christopher's, Scotty's, and Lisa 's ears are sewn into the dart seams on the head, or into the seams that join the head side pieces together.

8. The front side of the head and the assembled ear are placed with right sides of fabric together and stitched partway at the top to make floppy ears.

9. The front side and back side of the head are sewn together (top); the two parts before assembly (bottom).

10. Sew the chin seam and insert the head gusset between the side pieces.

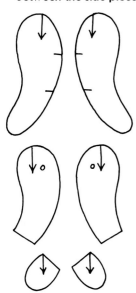

Sewing Floppy Ears

• Place the side of the head and the ear with right sides of fabric together and stitch as shown (Photo 8), but only up to the correct letter; do not sew into the seam allowance.

• Bend the ear, place the ear edge and the side of head together, and baste the ear in place to the side of the head.

• Now, sew the dart on the side of the head closed or, if the side is in two pieces, sew them together (Photo 9).

• Place the left and right side pieces of the head with right sides of fabric together and sew the chin seam. Pin and baste the head gusset in place. Make sure that the tip of the nose is lined up well with the chin seam (Photo 10). Stitch the seams.

• Turn the head right-side out.

If the above procedure for attaching ears in the seamline of the head seems too complicated, you may sew the ears by hand to the finished and stuffed head, wherever you want them (see page 29).

Arms

For each arm, you usually need one outer arm piece and one inner arm piece, and a paw, as shown in the diagram at left.

Note: Christopher and Benny, Ralph, Pearl, and Goldie do not have separate paw pieces.

Oscar's, Herbert's, Pete's, and Lisa's arms are made as described next.

• Pin the paw over the inner arm piece with right sides of fabric together and markings matched up (Photo 11, left) and sew the seam. Pin the seam allowances together in one direction (Photo 11, right).

- Pin the inner and outer arm pieces together accurately with right sides of fabric facing. Sew the seams, but remember to leave an opening for stuffing.

For Bartleby and Scotty, the arm consists of one arm piece and one paw piece (see drawing on this page). Assemble as follows:

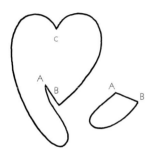

- Put the paw and arm pieces together with right sides facing and markings lined up (Photo 12, left), and stitch the straight seam (in the diagram on this page it's from A to B). Do not sew into the seam allowance beyond A.
- Carefully notch the seam allowance of the arm piece at A (Photo 12, right).
- Fold the arm piece in half, pin, and sew from A to C leaving an opening for stuffing (Photo 13, left).
- After the seam allowances have been notched, turn the arm right-side out (Photo 13, right).

11. Place paw over the inner arm, right sides together, and stitch (left). Pin the seam allowance in place and pin the unit to the outer arm (right).

12. For Bartleby and Scotty: Pin and stitch the paw to the arm; notch the seam allowance after stitching (right).

13. Fold the arm unit in half, sew it, and turn it right-side out.

14. Place the leg pieces together, pin, and sew.

15. Pin the sole in place and sew it to the leg unit.

16. If you want to, reinforce soles by gluing cardboard in place. (However, the bear will not be washable if it has cardboard soles.)

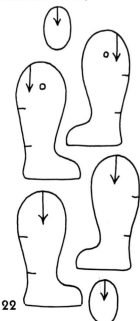

Legs

The basic leg is made from three pieces: one inner leg, one outer leg, and one sole (see diagram below, left). (Oscar and Pete are slightly different: each leg is made of only two pieces—one leg piece and one sole.) To make the basic leg:

- Put the inner and outer leg pieces with right sides of fabric facing, match the markings accurately, and sew together from the toe up around the top and down to the heel (Photo 14). Do not sew the lower, straight edge or the opening for stuffing.

- Pin the sole, with right side of fabric facing in, to the open foot of the leg unit, which is still inside out, and stitch it in place (Photo 15, left). Follow the pattern markings to position the sole in the opening. For a smaller bear, or for leather soles, it may be easier to hand-stitch the sole in place.

- If you want the sole to remain flat, rather than curving outwards when stuffed, glue a cardboard sole to the inside-out fur sole to reinforce it (Photo 16). Use the template for the sole and cut two cardboard soles without seam allowances. Do this before you turn the legs right-side out.

- Notch the seam allowances of the fabric, and glue the seam allowances to the cardboard.

- After the glue has dried, turn the leg right side out.

Body

The body consists of two front of body and two back of body pieces in most cases (see diagrams on page 23). **Exceptions:** Oscar is made from two body pieces. Ralph and Pete are also. Benny and Christopher are also made differently than the basic bear discussed below. The pattern for Brownie is completely different and is explained with that project.

Basic Bear Body Assembly

When you sew each body seam, start each seam at the neck end to avoid pulling and distorting the fabric.

- Put the front of body pieces together with right sides of fabric facing; pin them along the front centerline; and sew them together along that line to make the front of body unit.
- To make the back of body unit, pin and sew the back of body pieces together along the back centerline (Photo 17) in the same way, but leave an opening for stuffing.
- Pin the front of body unit to the back of body unit with right sides of fabric facing each other.
- Sew the front and back of body units together along the side seams, leaving an opening at the neck to insert the neck joint (Photo 18).

17. Two front body pieces (right) and two back body pieces (left) pinned and sewn together.

18. The front and back body pieces sewn together in one unit. The opening in the back seam was left for stuffing.

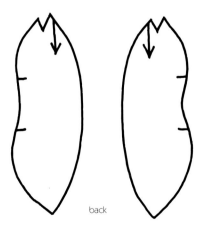

back

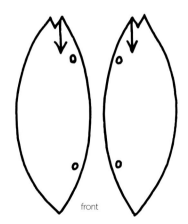

front

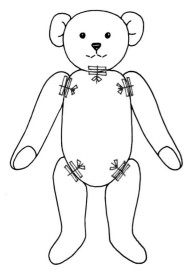

Placement of disk joints.

Inserting the Disk Joints

Suppliers offer complete joint sets of different sizes; the diameter of the disks you need varies, depending on the size of the bear. The correct joint size for each pattern is given in the list of materials. Below are a few important tips for inserting the joint mechanism. This is done before the limbs or body are stuffed.

- With a sharp, pointed scissors or an awl cut small holes into the fabric of the inner arm and inner leg pieces and on the body where the joints are marked on the pattern. Make sure that the holes accommodate but are not larger than the pin, screw, or cotter pin, whatever is used in your joint system.
- When you insert the disks, make sure that they are placed flat against the inside of the fabric.
- Install the joints and tighten them to a point where it takes effort to move them. The arms and legs will become more mobile again after the parts have been stuffed.

The different joint systems have already been discussed earlier. Below we describe how you install them.

Cotter-Pin Joints

The classic bear can be fitted, in true period fashion, with cotter-pin joints.

- Flatten the cotter pin loop to a T to keep it from being pulled through the washer. Slide a washer and a joint disk onto the cotter pin.
- Place the cotter pin with the disk joint inside an arm or leg; push the ends of the cotter pin through the joint hole in the fur to the outside of the arm or leg.
- Now, attach the limb to the body by pushing the cotter pin through the correct hole in the fur to the inside of the body.
- Slide the second joint disk and then the washer into place inside the bear's body and bend the ends of the cotter pin with needlenosed

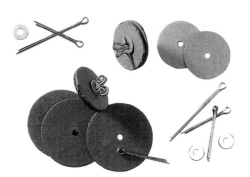

pliers into a snail shape or crown shape (see photo) against the washer to hold the limb in place.

Plastic Joints

- Slide the joint disk with the pin into the inside of the arm or leg, and feed the pin through the hole, made previously with an awl, to the outside of the arm or leg.
- Attach the arm or leg to its correct body place by sliding the pin

through the correct hole into the inside of the body; add the washer and secure it to the pin with the locking disk, inside the body.

- Check the proper placement of the limbs before snapping the locking disks in place.
- Push the locking disk as far as possible onto the pin. A combination pliers might be helpful for this step.

Screw Joints

- Slide a washer and a joint disk onto the screw.
- Slide the screw with washer and disk into the inside of an arm or leg; then feed the screw through the prepared hole to the outside of the limb (Photo 19).
- Attach the limb to the body by sliding the screw into the correct hole on the body fur; then slide a second joint disk and a washer over the screw, securing them with a wing-nut inside the body (see Photo 20).
- Check to see if all joints are in their proper places.
- Add a drop of epoxy resin glue or rapid drying glue between the screw and wing-nut to prevent the nut from loosening over time, but make sure that you do not get any glue on the fabric by mistake.
- Cover the spot where the glue has been applied with a little bit of stuffing material.

If you have the necessary tools at your workbench, you can make the joint disks yourself from plywood.

19. Placing the joint disks inside the arms and legs (screw joints).

20. Attaching the limbs to the body (screw joints).

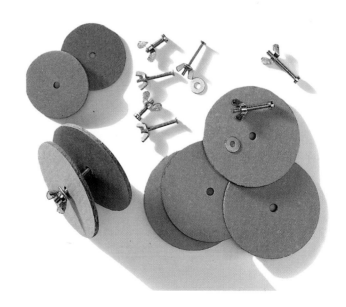

21. Mark the placement of the eyes with tacks or quilting pins.

22. Attach the eyes.

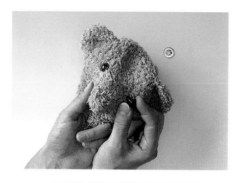

23. Run a line of basting stitches in strong thread along the neck edge; insert the disk joint.

24. Pull the basting thread tight and close the neck end with a few diagonal stitches.

Stuffing

The Head

- If you plan to use plastic safety eyes, they must be inserted before the head is stuffed, so they can be locked in place inside. (For attachment of other eyes, done after the head is fully stuffed, see page 31.)
- To plan placement of safety eyes, fill the head loosely with stuffing. Use pins with round plastic ends or tacks to try out various eye placements (Photo 21 and drawing on page 31).
- Mark the places you have chosen and cut a hole for each eye just big enough for the pin of the plastic eye to fit through.
- Remove the stuffing again, feed the pin through the fabric, and slide the locking disk as far as possible over the pin inside the head.

The head should be stuffed firmly so that it keeps its shape, especially the nose and the area around it.

- First, fill the head loosely.
- Next, concentrate on the nose area and push the stuffing firmly in place, starting at the chin seam and moving to the nose. Use a wooden stick or a wooden spoon handle.
- Use only a small amount of stuffing at a time, so you can shape the head the way you want, avoiding bulges or dents later.
- Continue to add stuffing until the head is as firm as a tennis ball, but the joint disk for the neck joint can still be placed—but just barely—into the neck opening.
- Next, take the joint disk and (depending on the joint system) add the washer on a cotter pin, screw, or a plastic disk with a pin.
- Place the joint disk (and washer, if

the system uses one) in the neck opening of the head with the cotter pin, screw, or pin extending to the outside (Photo 23).

- Run a line of basting stitches of strong thread around the neck edge of the head, ¼ inch (.5 cm) from the edge (Photo 23).
- Next, pull the thread around the neckline tight.
- Tie the neckline thread tightly, and secure the ends with diagonal stitches (see Photo 24).
- Attach the head to the body at the neck opening in the same manner described for the arms and legs (pp. 24–25). You can do this before or after the limbs are stuffed, but attach the head before you stuff the body.

Arms and Legs

- Stuff the limbs carefully and firmly, using small pieces of stuffing material; start at the feet and paws (Photo 25).
- Then, stuff the upper arm and leg areas and finish with the middle part of the arms and legs (pp. 24–25).
- Hand-stitch the opening closed with the mattress stitch (Photo 26). Use a long, strong upholstery needle and strong thread such as buttonhole thread or embroidery thread in a matching color.
- After about ⅔ of the opening has been closed, add more stuffing to avoid unsightly dents, if necessary.
- Finish closing the opening and carefully bury the ends of the thread inside the stuffing.

Body

- Loosely stuff the body with big chunks of stuffing material. Some people include a few pieces of fur fabric, so they will be available later in case repairs are needed.
- Continue to add stuffing, but use smaller pieces. Make sure that the areas around the joints, shoulders, neck, chest, tummy and crotch are stuffed very firm.

25. Stuff the limbs with stuffing material.

26. Stitch the stuffing openings closed by hand after stuffing, using the mattress stitch and strong thread.

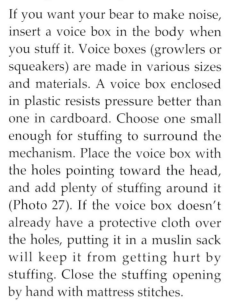

Giving the Teddy a Voice

If you want your bear to make noise, insert a voice box in the body when you stuff it. Voice boxes (growlers or squeakers) are made in various sizes and materials. A voice box enclosed in plastic resists pressure better than one in cardboard. Choose one small enough for stuffing to surround the mechanism. Place the voice box with the holes pointing toward the head, and add plenty of stuffing around it (Photo 27). If the voice box doesn't already have a protective cloth over the holes, putting it in a muslin sack will keep it from getting hurt by stuffing. Close the stuffing opening by hand with mattress stitches.

Inserting a Music Box

- If you want your teddy bear to have a music box, leave an opening of about 1¼ inches (3 cm) in the crotch of the body (between the legs) to insert the pull string of the music box.
- Stuff the body loosely. Then insert the music box; have the pull string extend outside the crotch opening (Photo 28). Sew up the crotch opening by hand, but only to a point where the pull string can still be pulled without having stuffing escape in the process.
- Continue adding stuffing, making sure that the music box is surrounded on all sides by stuffing so that you don't feel the box when you hold the bear.
- Before closing the stuffing opening, double-check to make sure that the music box is not pulled of place when the string is pulled.
- A Velcro seam closing lets you remove the music box when necessary—for instance, when the teddy bear has to get a "bath."
- If you are using Velcro, the seam allowance around the stuffing opening should be increased to at least 1 to 1¼ inches (2 to 3 cm), and should possibly be strengthened with interfacing. The Velcro closing will be covered later by the bear's clothes.

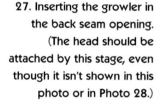

27. Inserting the growler in the back seam opening. (The head should be attached by this stage, even though it isn't shown in this photo or in Photo 28.)

28. A music box must be well cushioned by stuffing.

Attaching Ears by Hand*

Your bear's expression is determined by the size and placement of the ears (see below), the eyes (see page 31), and the snout (see page 30).

To give your bear some extra flair, turn the upper portion of the ear forward a bit, or add a pleat or small crease to the front part of the ear when sewing it to the head. Both ears should be equally far away from the tip of the nose. To make an ear:

- Place two ear pieces (ear and reverse) with right sides of fabric together; pin, baste, and sew the seams. Leave a small opening at the base of the ear for turning the ear right-side out. Notch the seam allowances (Photo 29).
- Trim off the excess seam allowance at the corners, turn the ear right-side out, shape the corners well and the rounded part. Add a bit of stuffing if desired.
- Tuck the seam allowance inside and sew the ear opening closed by hand with strong thread (Photo 29, right).

*See p. 20 for ears inserted in seamline.

29. Left: two ear pieces sewn together with right sides facing; seam allowance notched. Right: the seam allowance is tucked in and the seam is closed with strong thread.

30. The ears are sewn to the head.

- Pin the ears in the area of the darts (if there are darts on the head) and hand-sew them on with strong thread and the mattress stitch (Photo 30).

Various ways of shaping ears.

29

Embroidering the Snout

Carefully trim down the pile around the nose with a pair of sharp-pointed scissors, e.g, a cuticle scissors or mustache scissors, before embroidering, if you wish (see Photo 34).

- For the nose, take a long piece of embroidery thread and a long embroidery needle.
- Put the needle in at either the back or the side of the head; pull the needle out at the tip of the nose. Using vertical or horizontal stitches, embroider the nose with closely placed stitches (drawings 1 to 3). See suggestions at left.
- If necessary, finish the edges by sewing edge stitches across the stitches used to make the nose (drawing 4).
- Bring the needle out at the center seam, directly below the nose (drawing 5); embroider the mouth with a few stitches (drawings 6 to 10). The mouth shape determines if your bear is happy or sad.
- Bring the needle with the rest of the thread through the head to the starting point and tie the thread with the first thread end.
- Thread both thread ends through the needle, pull them into the head, pull out the needle again, and trim off any excess thread.

Attaching Sew-On Eyes

Traditional bears had glass or shoe-button eyes, sewn on the stuffed head. Glass eyes come attached to wires. Some wires are already looped. Some you must bend yourself with needlenosed pliers. Replicas of shoe-button eyes and other plastic eyes are also available. They are sewn to the head with strong thread, such

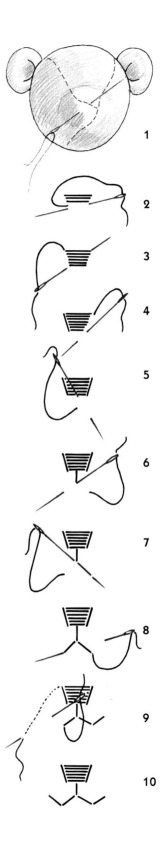

as carpet or buttonhole thread, and a long needle (7 to 10 inches, or 17 to 25 cm).

Eye placement is important for your bear's expression. Using two straight pins with colored heads, experiment with different eye positions and choose one that suits you.

- Using a sufficiently long piece of doubled thread, make a loop around the wire loop and carefully flatten the wire loop with flat-nosed pliers (Photo 31).

- At the place where the eye is to be attached, separate the weave slightly with a blunt-tipped needle, creating a small hole.

- Feed one end of the thread that has been pulled through the loop through the eye of a long needle; push the needle through the small hole in the weave and out at the opposite side of the head. Do the same with the other end of the thread (Photo 32). Leave a $1/8$ inch (2 to 3 mm) space between the places on the back of the head where the thread ends exit.

- Check eye placement again; then pull the two ends of the thread tight until the eye cannot be moved. The wire loops will completely disappear inside the head.

- Knot the thread ends together and pull them inside the head.

31. Loop the thread through the wire loop of the eye and flatten the wire loop with pliers.

32. Mark the position of the eyes, widen the weave at those places with a blunt-tipped needle, and sew on the eyes.

- See how different eye placements change the expression. You can pull the two ends of the thread together at the neckline, ears, or below the chin. If you have difficulty holding or pulling the needle through, use a combination pliers.

Various eye placements.

33. Embroidering claws.

34. If you wish, you can trim the area around the nose.

35. Suitable clothing makes a bear look stylish.

REMINDER
The patterns do not include seam allowances; therefore, add ³⁄₈ inch (1 cm) around the patterns for the seam allowances (except at folds) and ³⁄₄ inch (2 cm) for the hems of sleeves, dresses, jackets, and pants legs.

Embroidering the Claws
You can give your teddy bears claws. With the same thread used for the nose and mouth, make 3 or 4 stitches (Photo 33). Secure the thread ends in the fabric.

Shaving
To shave your teddy bear, start at the tip of the nose and carefully cut the pile close to the base of the fabric with a pair of sharp cuticle scissors, "shaving" as little or as much as you like (Photo 34). Brush the teddy bear.

Clothing
We have supplied a set of clothing for each bear. These patterns can be adjusted or altered to suit your fancy, providing your teddy bear with a perfect wardrobe.
• Pants, jackets, pullovers, and dresses are to some extent interchangeable between bears (but check the measurements).
• Enlarge or reduce a pattern on a photocopier to fit the bear.
• Solid-color or small-print fabrics work best for a bear's wardrobe.

Sewing Terms and Markings
Gathering. With the sewing machine set for a long stitch, machine-baste a row of stitches above and one below the seamline where marked for gathering on the pattern. Pull both lower threads at the same time until the gathered part fits the pattern. Tie the upper and lower thread together and distribute the gathers equally.
Nap and Straight Grain. The large arrow on each pattern piece indicates the direction of the nap (fur fabrics) or the straight grain of the fabric

(other fabrics), which always runs parallel to the selvage edge of the fabric. (See page 16 to 17 for nap and pattern placement.)

Interfacing. Iron-on interfacing is stiff and has adhesive on one side. It is designed to strengthen lightweight and stretchable fabrics. When cutting interfacing, include the seam allowance. The interfacing is ironed onto the wrong side (back) of the fabric on a low setting (follow the manufacturer's instructions). Let the material cool after applying.

Letters. Letters of the alphabet on the pattern indicate where two pieces of pattern or fabric are joined. The same letters should always be aligned accurately. Some pattern pieces are given in two parts. In that case, follow the bear's instructions and join the pattern pieces before cutting the templates or fabric.

Foldlines. For clothing, place the edge of a pattern piece marked with a foldline symbol on doubled fabric. If there are two foldlines at right angles on a pattern, place them on fabric folded in fourths before cutting.

However, thick fabric such as fur fabric can't be cut on the fold. In that case, trace the pattern and its mirror image onto a folded piece of tracing paper. Transfer all marks to both halves of the pattern paper and make a template. Trace the full template onto the back of the fur fabric. Don't add a seam allowance to any foldline sides of a pattern.

Basting stitch.

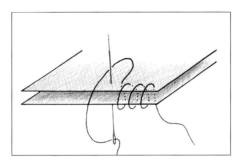

Overcasting stitch.

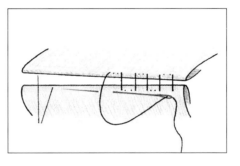

Mattress stitch.

Key to Symbols and Terms

Cut 2 (1 R): Cut one with the pattern facing up and one with the pattern turned face down on the fabric

A- - - -> A: Fold so A lies over A

– – – – : Stitching line

> < : Leave space between the arrows open to add stuffing

- - - - - : Joining line for two pattern parts (do this before cutting fabric)

—> (large arrow): Direction of nap (fur fabric) or straight grain of fabric (other fabrics)

—.—.— : Align fold of fabric here

|- - - -| : Gather here

OSCAR AND HIS FRIENDS

OSCAR

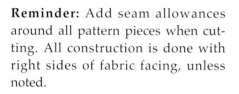 *Oscar*

at 24 inches tall (60 cm), is the tallest teddy bear in this book. He was made from high-quality synthetic plush and has leather paws. Dressed up as a cook, he cuts a particularly striking figure.

Reminder: Add seam allowances around all pattern pieces when cutting. All construction is done with right sides of fabric facing, unless noted.

The Bear

Before cutting fabric: Some pattern pieces are given in two parts. Join them as follows before making templates and cutting fabric:
- Head gusset: Join parts 1 and 2 along line E–D.
- Body: Join pattern parts 1 and 2 along line H–I.
- Leg: Join pattern parts 1 and 2 along line K–L. Trace pattern on folded paper and open out for whole leg.

Oscar: Pieces to Cut
Front side of head: cut 1 (1 R)
Back side of head: cut 2 (1 R)
Head gusset: cut 1
Sole: cut 2
Ears: cut 4 (2 R)
Body: cut 2 (1 R)
Outer arm: cut 2 (1 R)
Inner arm: cut 2 (1 R)
Paw: cut 2
Leg: cut 2 (1 R) of whole leg. Mark on the fabric where the leg joint goes.

Sewing Instructions for Bear
Follow instructions as described in the chapter on basic techniques.
- Stitch the ears into the seam along line B–C when stitching the front and back side of head pieces.
- Stitch the leather paws to the inner arms with running stitches about $\frac{1}{32}$ inch (1 mm) in from the edge, before the inner and outer arm are sewn together.

MATERIALS FOR BEAR
- 24 × 54 in (.6 × 1.4 m) yellow synthetic plush with woven backing
- 8 × 10 in (.2 × .25 m) leather for paws and soles
- pair of glass eyes, 16 mm size
- 1 joint set for a 24 in tall (60 cm) bear
- 2.2 lb (1 kg) stuffing
- sewing thread
- small amount of brown wool yarn
- strong thread
- growler

Oscar's Jacket

Before cutting fabric: Lengthen the front and back jacket pattern pieces by 2¾ in (7 cm). Join parts 1 and 2 of sleeve pattern at E–F.

Jacket Pieces to Cut
Jacket front: cut 2 (1 R).
Jacket back: cut 1 on folded fabric
Sleeve: cut 2 (1 R).
Collar: cut 1 on fabric folded in fourths.

Sewing the Jacket
- Fold and stitch in place the pleat on the jacket back. Fold the self-facing of the jacket front pieces in and baste in place. Pin and stitch the front and back jacket pieces together at the shoulder seams.
- Stitch the sleeves to the armholes, aligning the G's.
- Pin the jacket front and back together at the side seams; pin the sides of each sleeve together. Sew the jacket side seams and sleeve seams.
- Fold the collar along the long foldline (wrong side out); stitch the short sides closed.
- Turn the collar right side out and pin one long side on the outside of the jacket at the neck opening with raw edges of the jacket neck and collar aligned, aligning letters K and L. Stitch the seam. Press the rest of the collar up, turn the seam allowance under on the unattached long side, and hand-stitch to the inside of the neck opening.
- Hem sleeves and the jacket's lower edge. Sew buttons as indicated and make buttonholes on the front.

Oscar's Pants

Before cutting fabric: Join pants front pattern part 1 to pants front pattern part 2 along line C–D. Join pants back pattern part 1 to part 2 along A–B.

Pants Pieces to Cut
Pants front: cut 2 (1 R).
Pants back: cut 2 (1 R).

Sewing the Pants
- Pin the pants front pieces at the front centerline and stitch the center seam. Pin the pants back pieces together at the back centerline and stitch the back center seam.
- Put the front and back pants units together and stitch the inner and outside seams of the front to the back. Fold the waistband in at the foldline and stitch on the stitching line to make the elastic casing; leave 1 inch (2.5 cm) opening to thread the elastic through and insert it.

Oscar's Hat

Hat Pieces to Cut
Hat piece 1 and 2: cut 1 of each on fabric folded in quarters.
Cut hat piece 2 of interfacing fabric also.

Sewing the Hat
- To make the hatband, fuse the interfacing to the wrong side of hat piece 2. Fold it in half on its length with right sides facing and stitch the short sides (M–N–M) together. Turn the band right-side out. Baste the long open sides together.
- Run two lines of long stitches around the outer edge of hat piece 1; pull them up until the outside is about 15¾ in (40 cm). With right sides of fabric facing, pin its raw edges to the raw edge of piece 2, arranging the gathers to fit. Stitch piece 1 to piece 2.

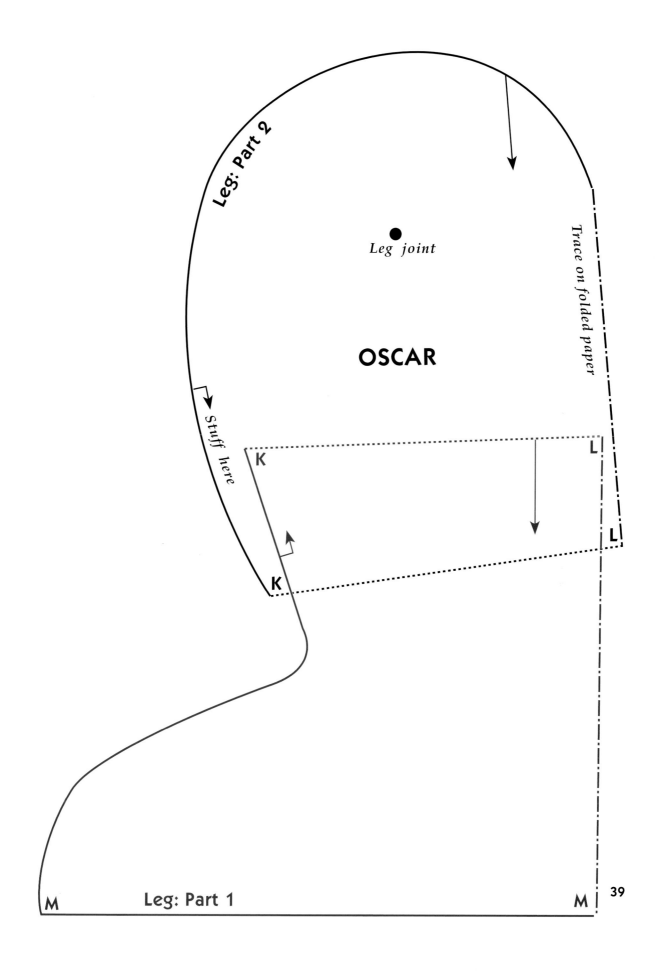

Leg: Part 2

Leg joint

Trace on folded paper

OSCAR

Stuff here

K

K

L

L

Leg: Part 1

M

M

39

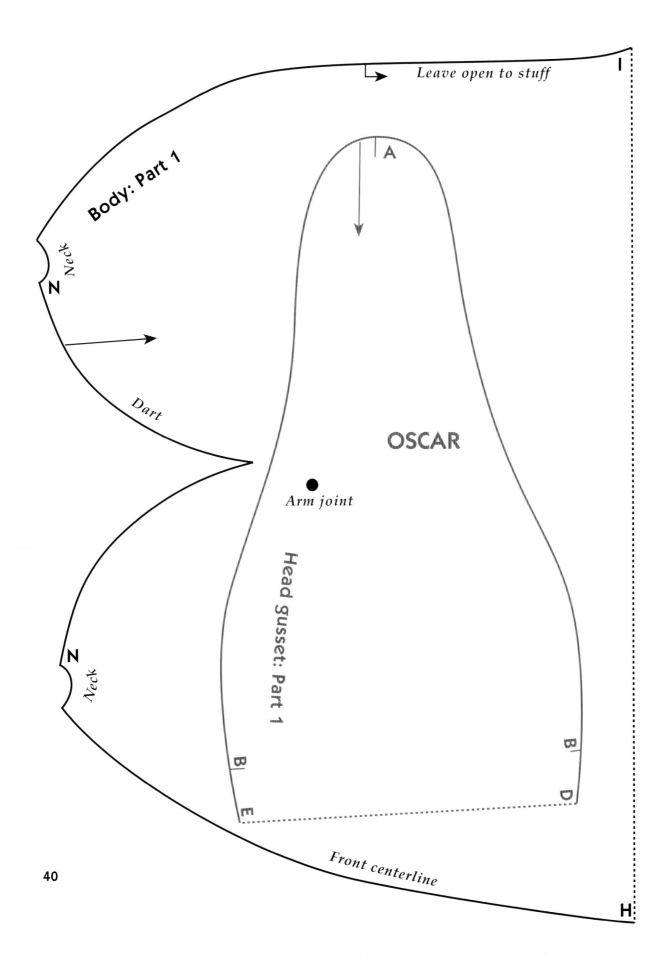

Body: Part 1

Neck

Z

Dart

Neck

Z

Leave open to stuff

A

OSCAR

●
Arm joint

Head gusset: Part 1

B|

B|

D

E

Front centerline

I

H

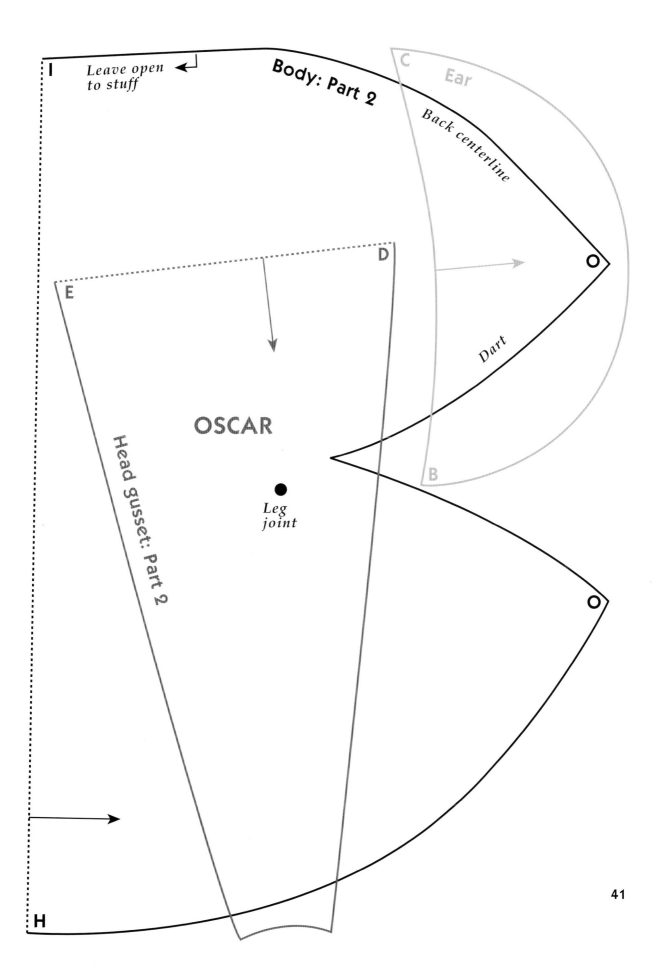

I

Leave open to stuff

Body: Part 2

C

Ear

Back centerline

D

E

O

Dart

B

OSCAR

Head gusset: Part 2

●
Leg joint

O

41

H

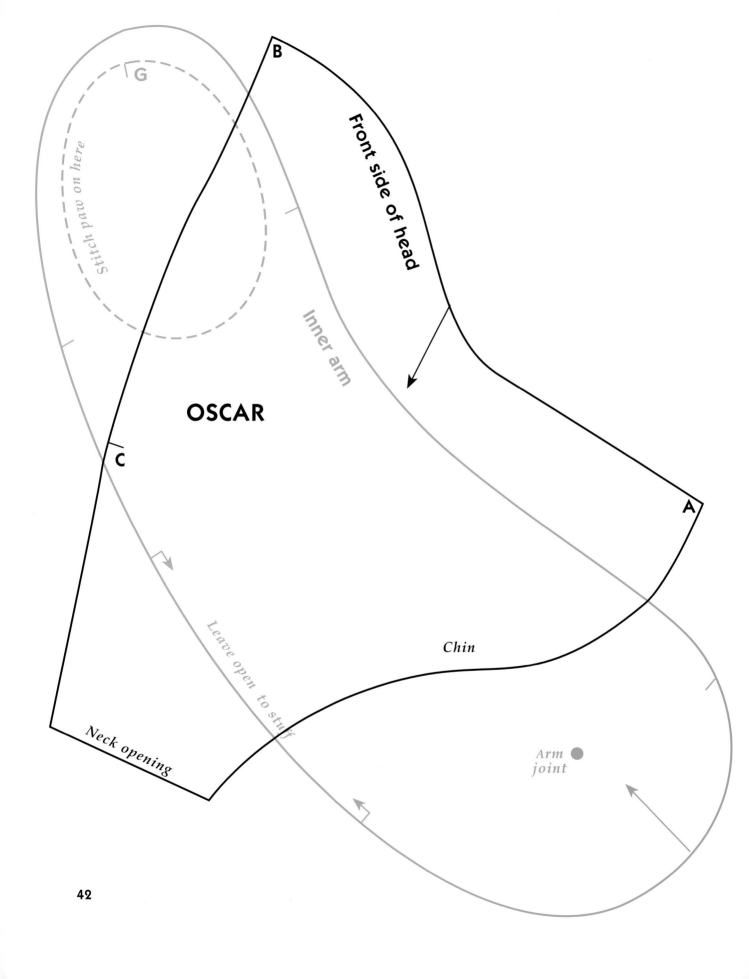

B

Front side of head

G

Stitch paw on here

Inner arm

OSCAR

C

Chin

Arm
joint

Leave open to stuff

Neck opening

A

42

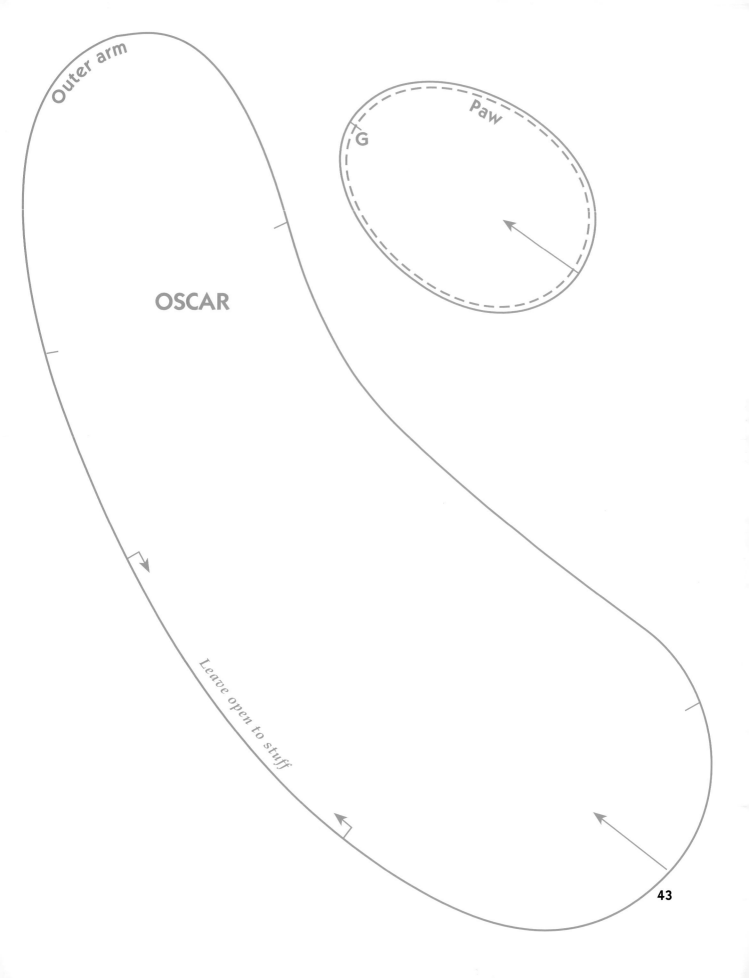

Outer arm

Paw

G

OSCAR

Leave open to stuff

43

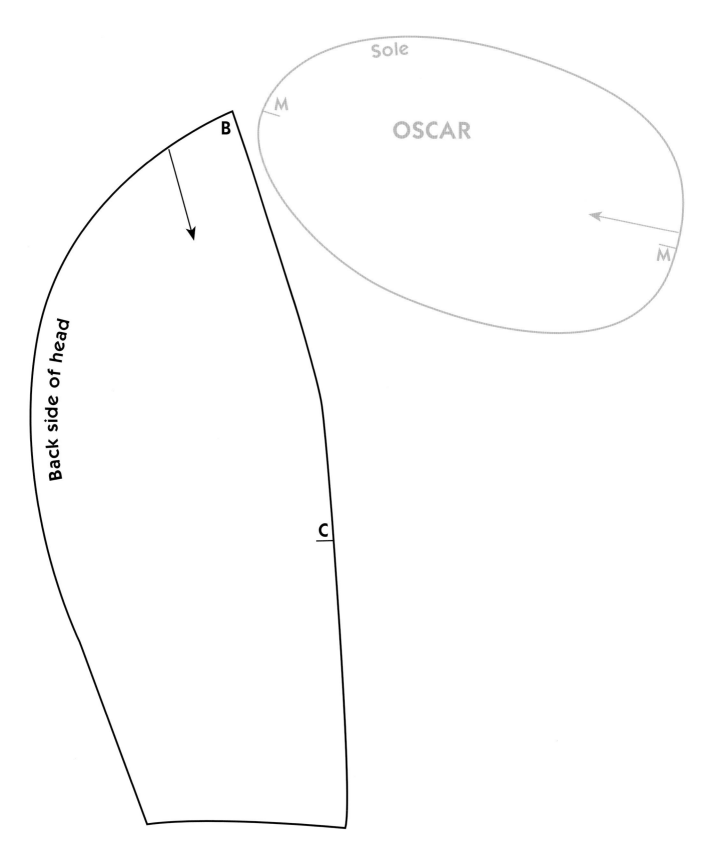

Sole

M

OSCAR

M

B

Back side of head

C

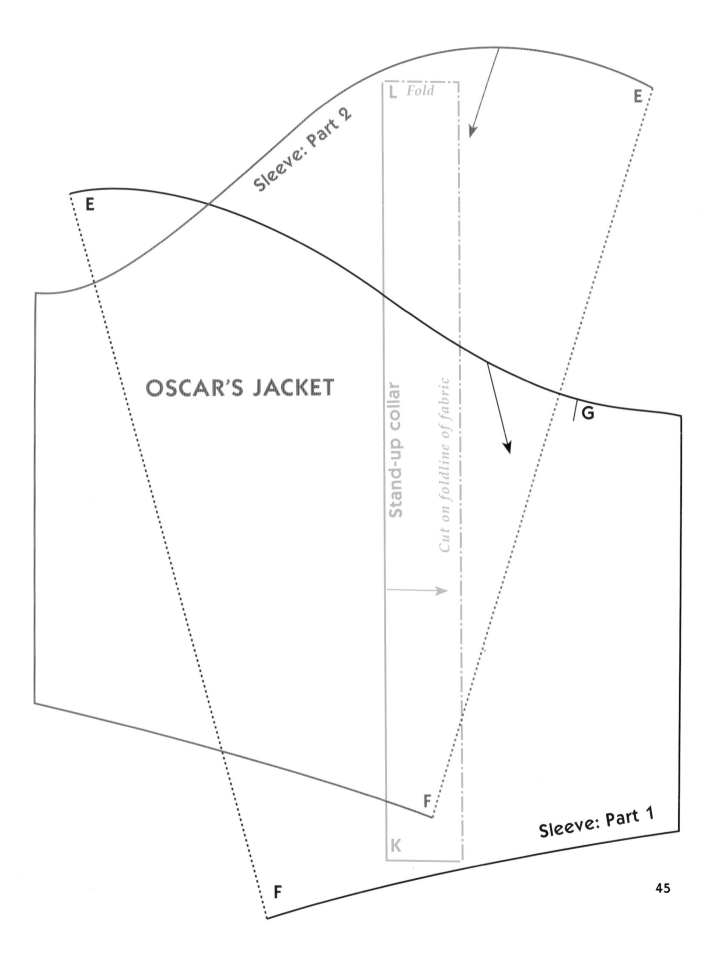

Sleeve: Part 2

E

E

OSCAR'S JACKET

Stand-up collar

Cut on foldline of fabric

L *Fold*

G

F

K

F

Sleeve: Part 1

45

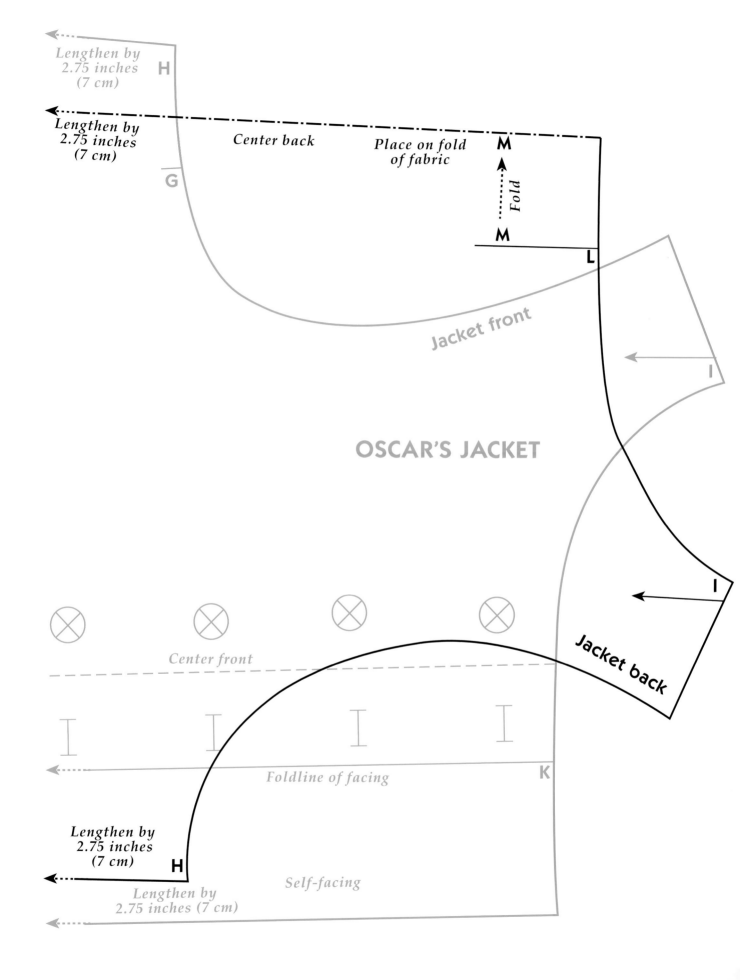

Lengthen by
2.75 inches
(7 cm)

H

Lengthen by
2.75 inches
(7 cm)

Center back

Place on fold
of fabric

M

Fold

M

L

G

Jacket front

I

OSCAR'S JACKET

I

Jacket back

Center front

Foldline of facing

K

Lengthen by
2.75 inches
(7 cm)

H

Self-facing

Lengthen by
2.75 inches (7 cm)

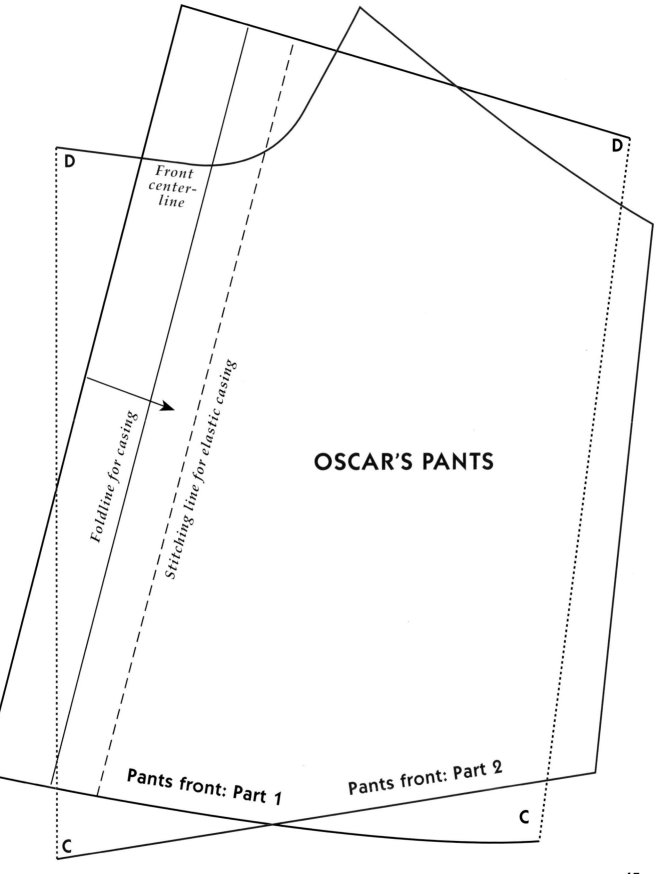

D

Front
center-
line

D

Foldline for casing

Stitching line for elastic casing

OSCAR'S PANTS

Pants front: Part 1

Pants front: Part 2

C

C

47

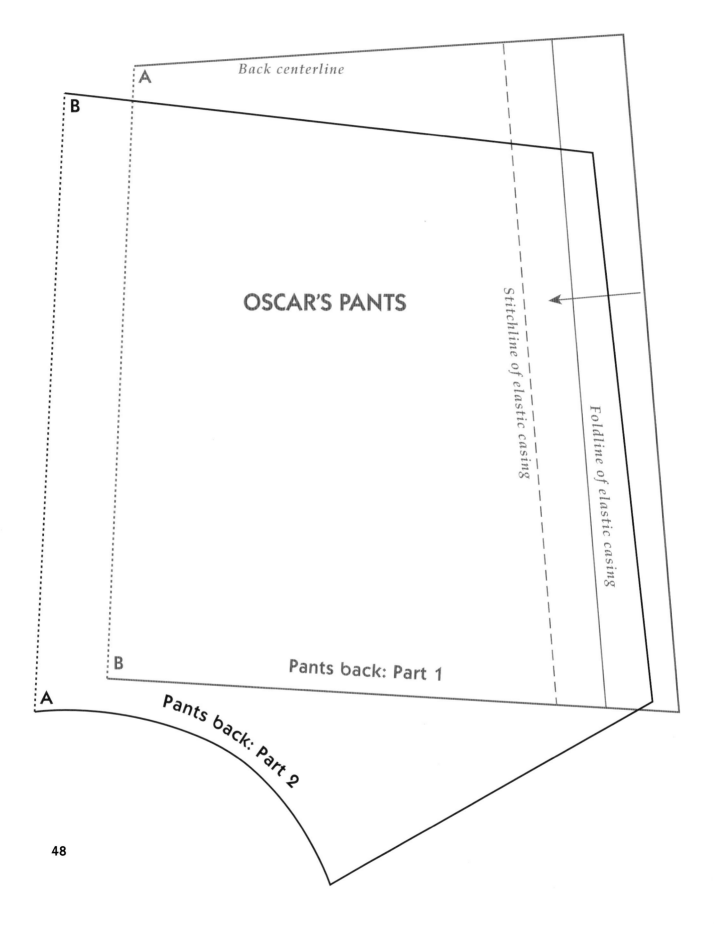

Back centerline

A

B

Stitchline of elastic casing

Foldline of elastic casing

OSCAR'S PANTS

B

Pants back: Part 1

A

Pants back: Part 2

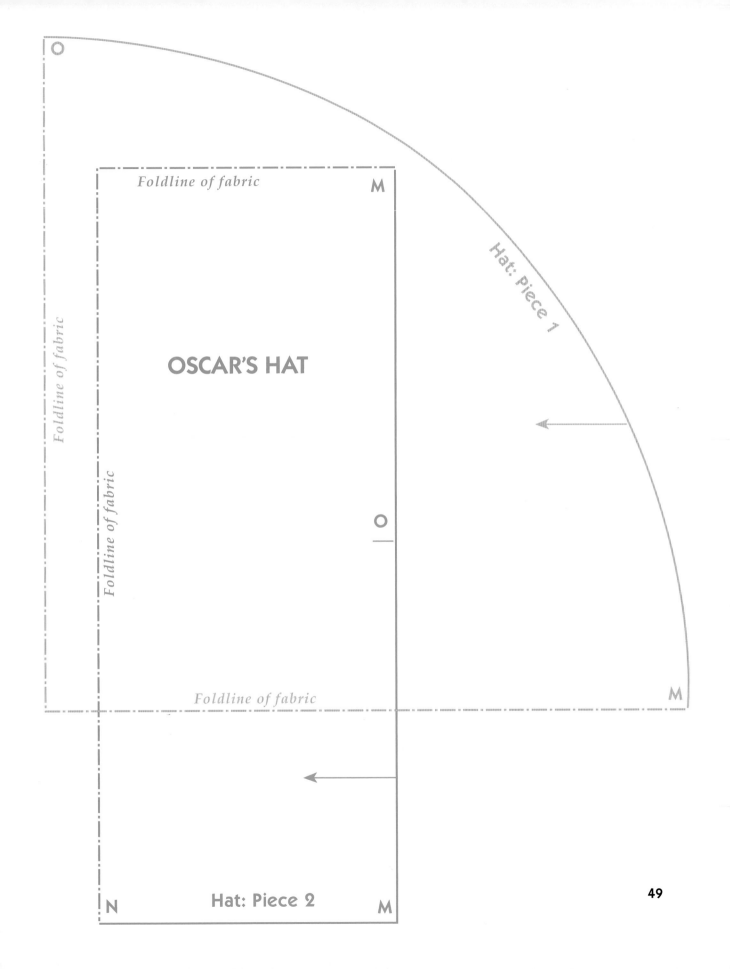

O

Foldline of fabric

Foldline of fabric

M

Foldline of fabric

OSCAR'S HAT

Hat: Piece 1

O

Foldline of fabric

M

N   Hat: Piece 2   M

HERBERT

Herbert

stands 19½ inches (50 cm) tall. He was the model for all the step-by-step photos, and you may see the exact steps taken to create him in the chapter on basic techniques.

Reminder: Add seam allowances around all pattern pieces when cutting. Construction is done with right sides of fabric facing, unless noted.

Before cutting fabric: Some pattern pieces are given in 2 parts. Join them as follows before making templates and cutting fabric:

- Head gusset: Join parts 1 and 2 along line B–C.
- Front of body: Join parts 1 and 2 along line K–L.
- Back of body: Join parts 1 and 2 along line M–N.

The Bear

Herbert: Pieces to Cut

Side of head: cut 2 (1 R)
Head gusset: cut 1
Ears: cut 4 (2 R)
Front of body: cut 2 (1 R)
Back of body: cut 2 (1 R)
Outer arm: cut 2 (1 R)
Inner arm: cut 2 (1 R)
Paw: cut 2 (1 R)
Outer leg: cut 2 (1 R)
Inner leg: cut 2 (1 R)
Sole: cut 2

Sewing Instructions for Bear

Follow instructions as described in the chapter on basic techniques. Sew the ears by hand on the finished and stuffed head (see page 29), aligning at E.

MATERIALS FOR BEAR

- ☐ 20 in × 54 in (.5 × 1.4 m) curly yellow mohair plush (woven backing)
- ☐ 8 in × 8 in (.2 m × .2 m) leather (paws/soles)
- ☐ pair of glass eyes, 16 mm size
- ☐ joint set for a 19½ inch (50 cm) tall bear
- ☐ 29 oz (800 g) stuffing
- ☐ sewing thread
- ☐ black wool for nose
- ☐ strong thread
- ☐ growler

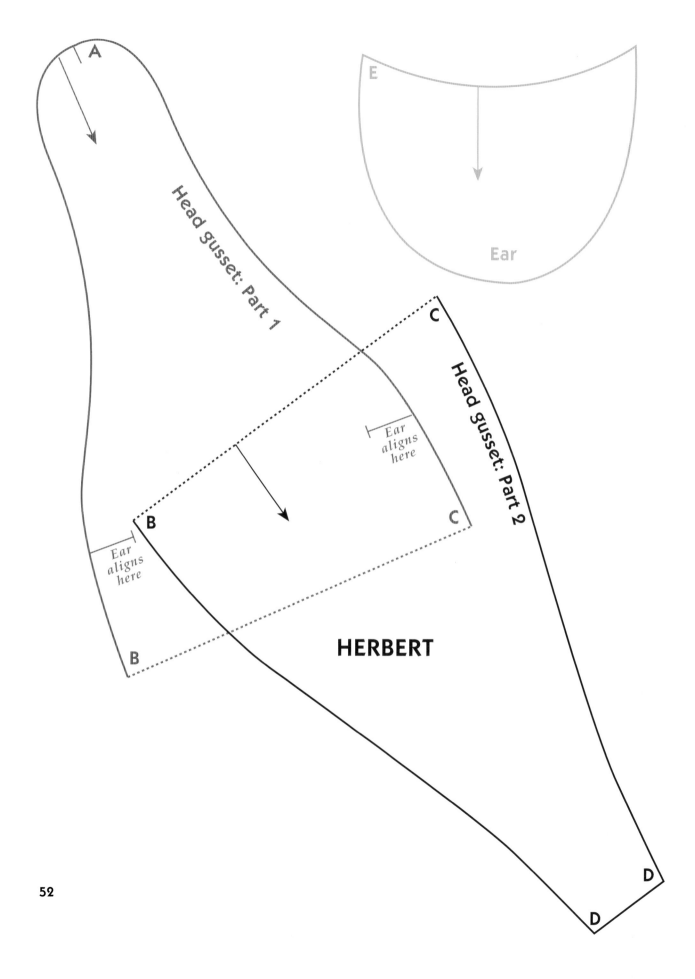

A

Head gusset: Part 1

E

Ear

C

Ear aligns here

C

Head gusset: Part 2

B

Ear aligns here

B

HERBERT

D

D

Herbert's Hooded Shirt

Before cutting fabric: Join the following pattern pieces:

- Shirt front: Join parts 1 and 2 along line A–B.
- Shirt back: Join parts 1 and 2 along line C–D.
- Hood: Join parts 1 and 2 along line E–F. Add ³⁄₈ in (2 cm) seam allowance to hood at front edge.

Shirt Pieces to Cut
Shirt front: cut 2 (1 R)
Shirt back: cut 1 on folded fabric
Hood: cut 2 (1 R)

Sewing the Shirt
- Pin the shirt front pieces together and stitch the center seam from the arrow down to the lower edge.
- Pin the shirt front and back pieces together and stitch the shoulder and side seams.
- Pin hood pieces and stitch together along the back center seam. Stitch darts closed on the hood.
- To make the drawstring casing, fold in the seam allowance of the front edge of the hood and stitch it down, leaving a small opening to insert the drawstring near G.
- Turn the self-facings of the shirt front seams in and stitch.
- Stitch the hood to the neck of the shirt, aligning them at G.
- Hem sleeves and shirt bottom and insert the cord in its casing.

Herbert's Pants

Before cutting fabric: Join the following pattern parts:

- Pants front: Join parts 1 and 2 along line A–B.
- Pants back: Join parts 1 and 2 along line C–D.

Pants Pieces to Cut
Pants front: cut 2 (1 R)
Pants back: cut 2 (1 R)

Sewing the Pants
- Pin the pants front pieces together and stitch along the front center seamline.
- Pin the pants back pieces together and stitch along the back center seamline.
- Stitch the front and back pants sections together along the inner leg seams and outside seams.
- Turn the self-facing in at the waist and sew along the stitching line, leaving a small opening to insert an elastic, and insert it.
- Hem pants. Sew on buttons for the suspenders.

Herbert's Cap

Pattern Pieces to Cut
Cap top: cut 8
Visor: cut 2
Headband: cut 1 on folded fabric

Sewing the Cap
- Stitch the two visor pieces together along the rounded edge; turn right-side out.
- Take two cap top pieces; stitch together from A to B. Stitch on a third from A to B on the second side of the first piece. Add pieces until you complete the circle and use all 8 pieces. Clip seam allowances at curves. Run 2 lines of basting stitches to gather cap along the edge; pull up to 16 in (40 cm).
- Sew on visor, aligning at C, on the outside. Stitch the headband to the outside of the cap and then turn it in and hand-baste it inside.

MATERIALS
Herbert's Hooded Shirt
- 13.5 in × 58.5 in (.35 m × 1.5 m) velour
- 1 yard (.9 m) cord for drawstring

Herbert's Pants
- 13.5 in × 35 in (.35 m × .9 m) cotton fabric
- 6 small buttons
- about 18 in (.45 m) waistband elastic
- doll-size suspenders

Herbert's Cap
- 8 in × 54 in (.2 m × 1.4 m) cotton fabric
- 6 in × 20 in (.15 m × .5 m) iron-on interfacing

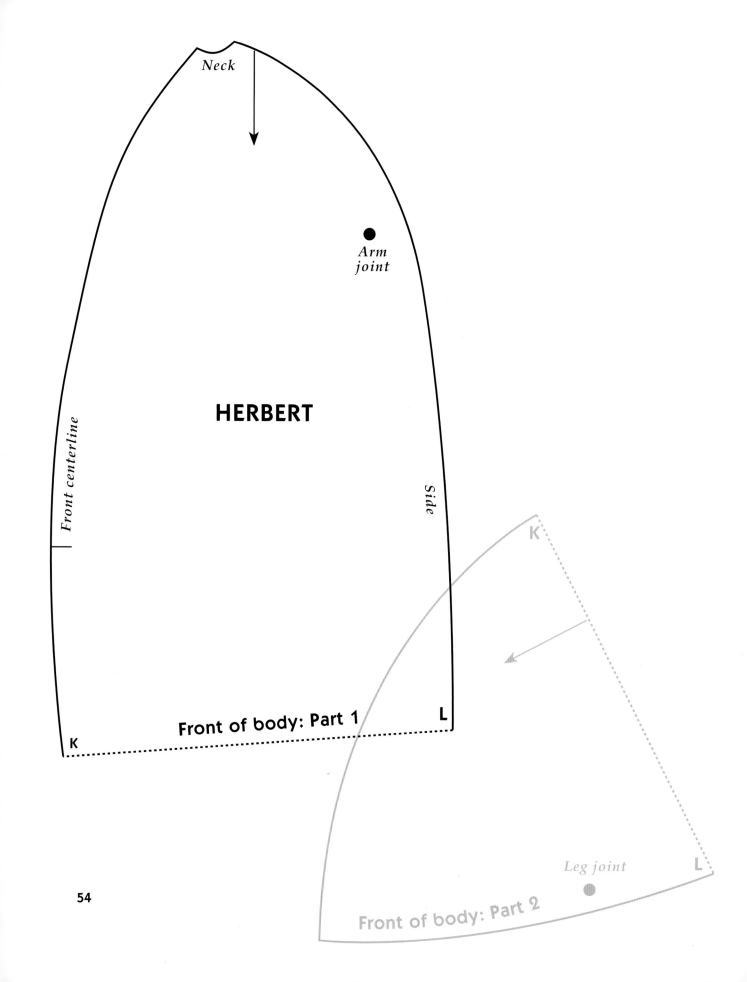

Neck

●
Arm joint

Front centerline

HERBERT

Side

K

Front of body: Part 1

L

K

L

Leg joint

Front of body: Part 2

54

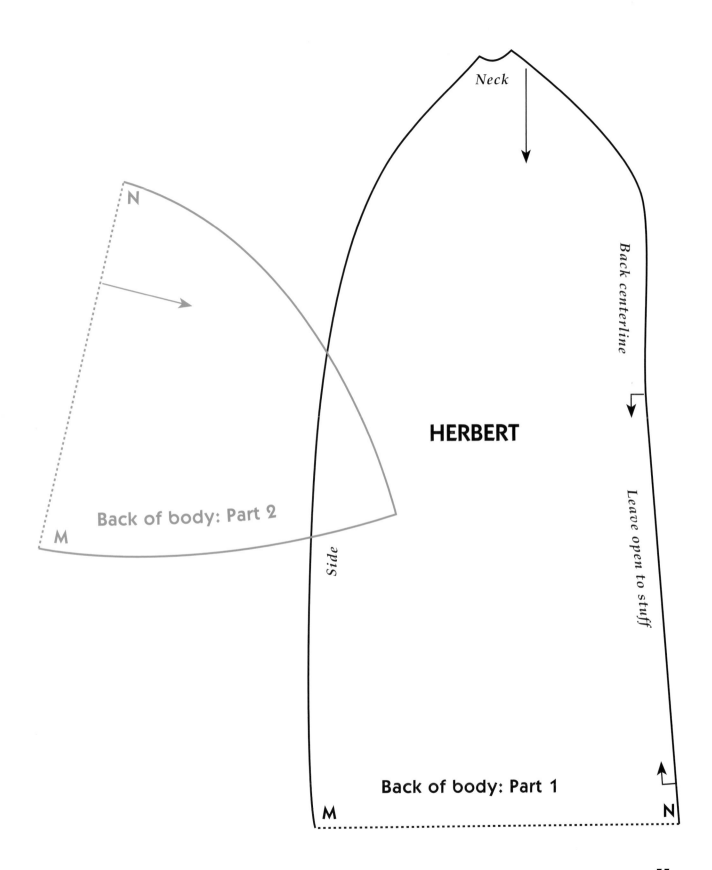

Neck

Back centerline

HERBERT

Leave open to stuff

Side

N

Back of body: Part 2

M

M   Back of body: Part 1   N

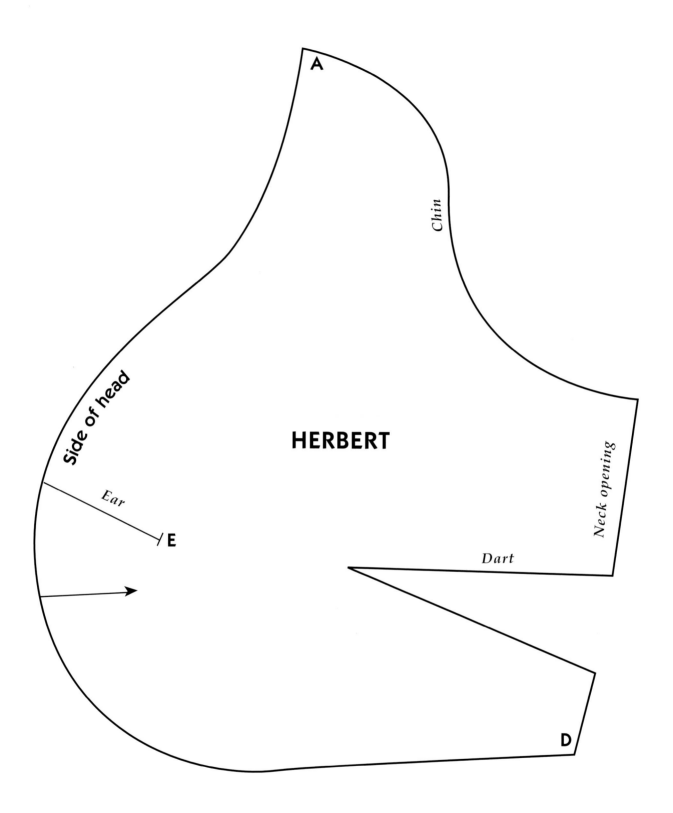

A

Chin

Side of head

HERBERT

Neck opening

Ear

Dart

E

D

56

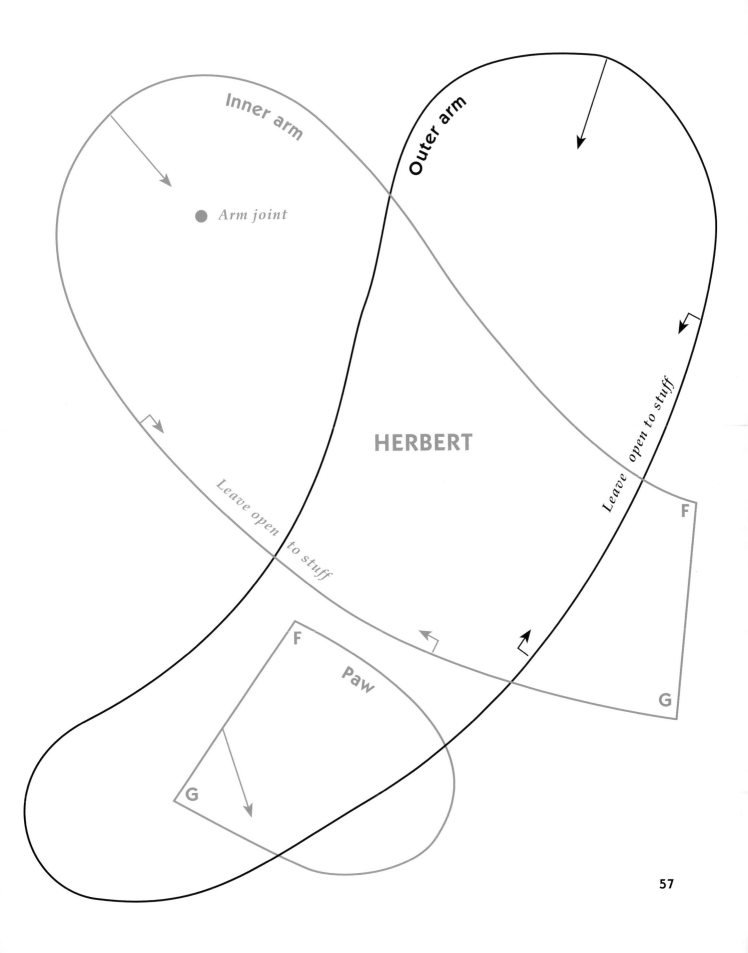

Inner arm

Outer arm

● Arm joint

HERBERT

Leave open to stuff

Leave open to stuff

F

G

F

Paw

G

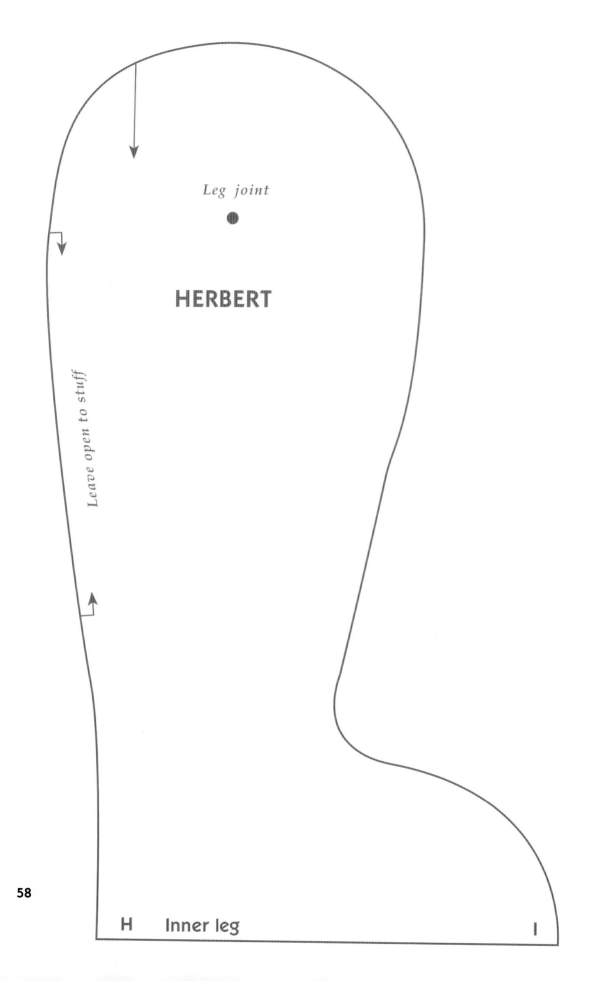

Leg joint

HERBERT

Leave open to stuff

58

H Inner leg I

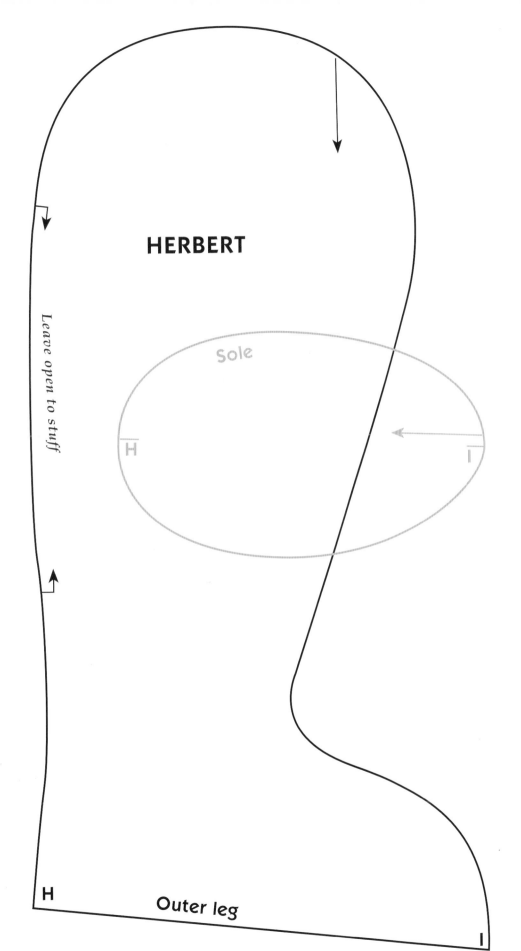

HERBERT

Leave open to stuff

Sole

H

I

H

Outer leg

I

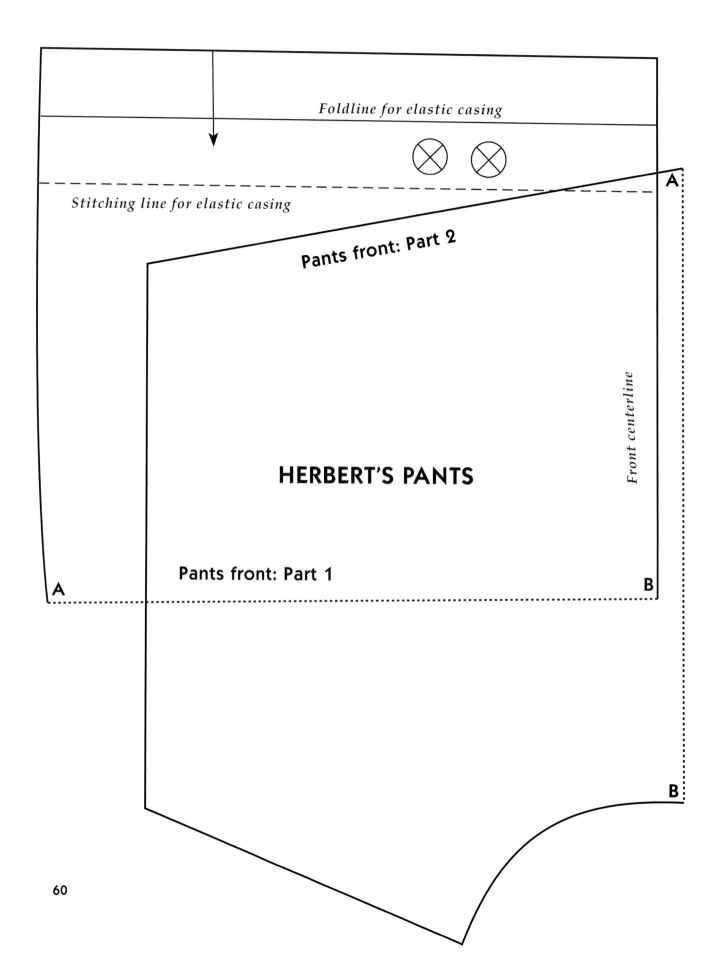

Foldline for elastic casing

Stitching line for elastic casing

Pants front: Part 2

HERBERT'S PANTS

Front centerline

Pants front: Part 1

A

B

A

B

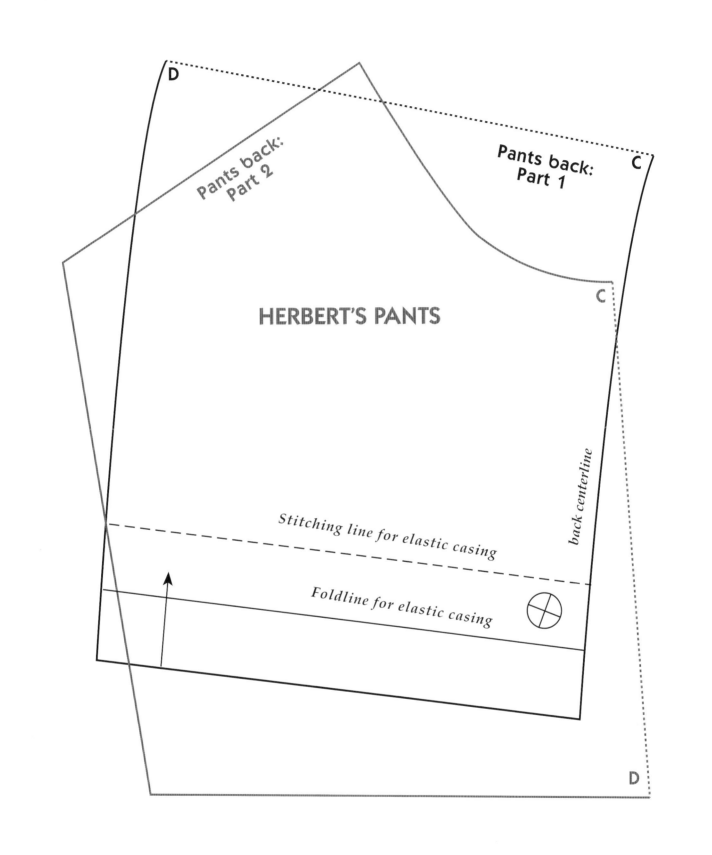

D

Pants back:
Part 2

Pants back:
Part 1

C

HERBERT'S PANTS

C

back centerline

Stitching line for elastic casing

Foldline for elastic casing

D

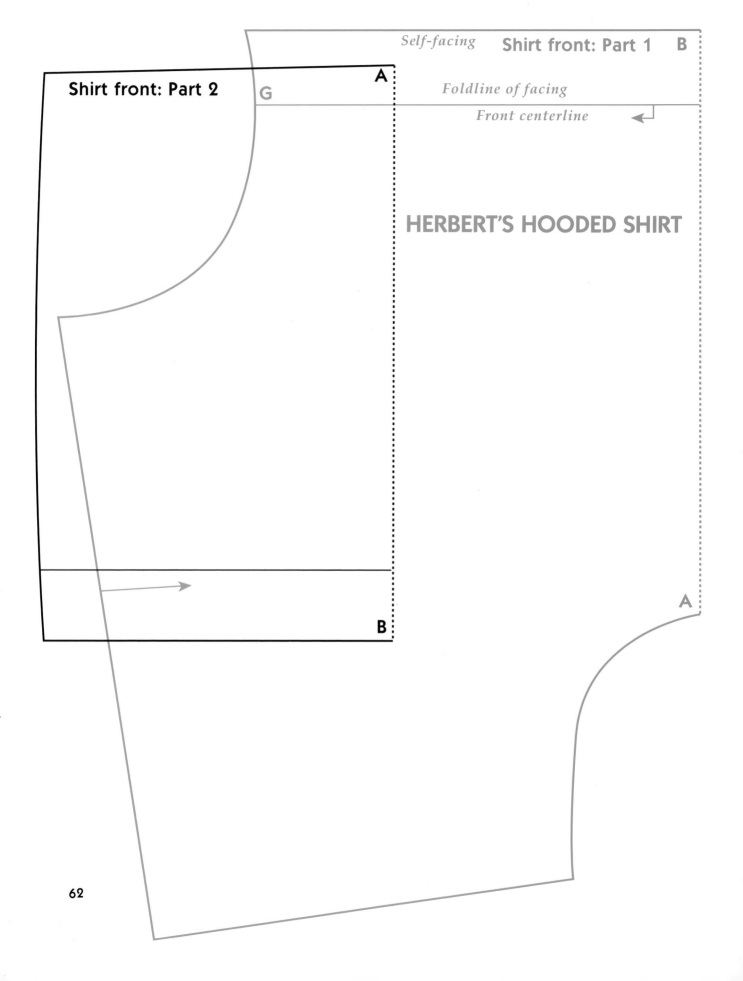

Self-facing   **Shirt front: Part 1**   B

A

G   *Foldline of facing*

Shirt front: Part 2

Front centerline

HERBERT'S HOODED SHIRT

B

A

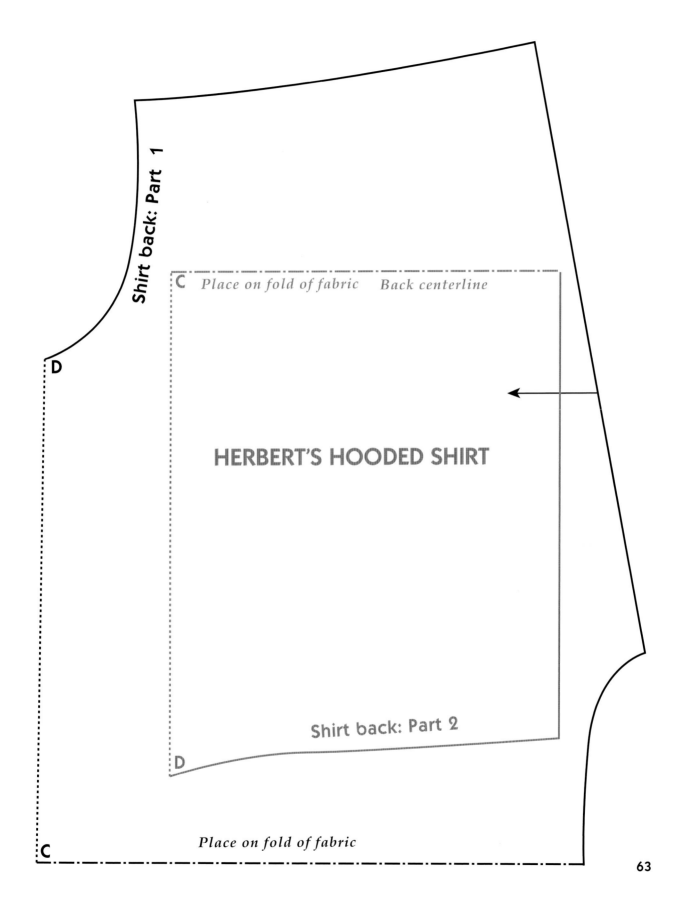

Shirt back: Part 1

D

C *Place on fold of fabric*   *Back centerline*

HERBERT'S HOODED SHIRT

Shirt back: Part 2

D

Place on fold of fabric

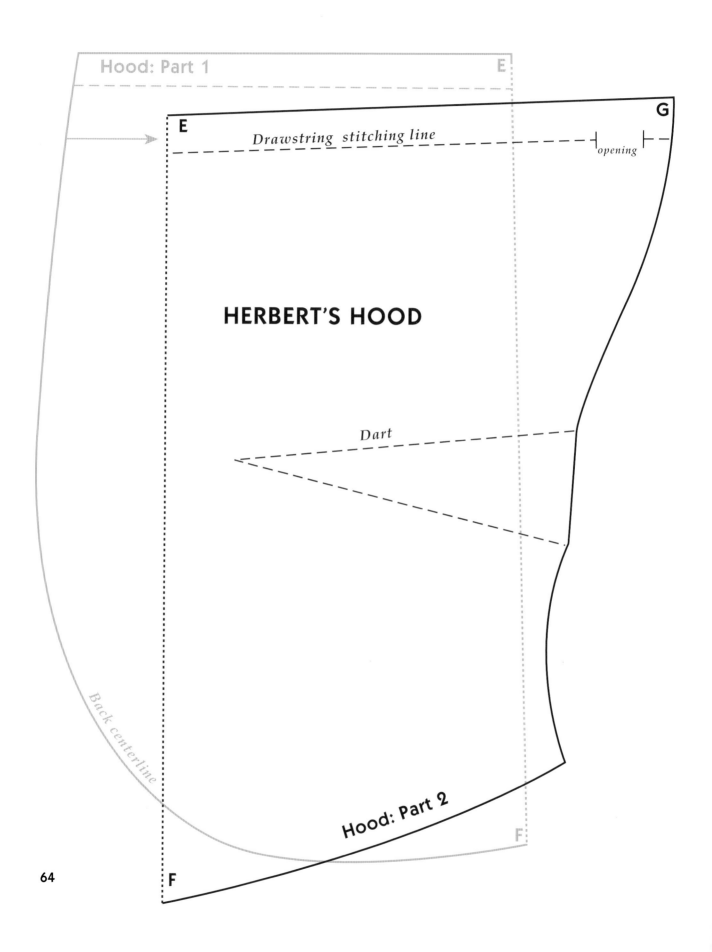

Hood: Part 1

E

E

Drawstring stitching line

opening

G

HERBERT'S HOOD

Dart

Back centerline

Hood: Part 2

F

F

64

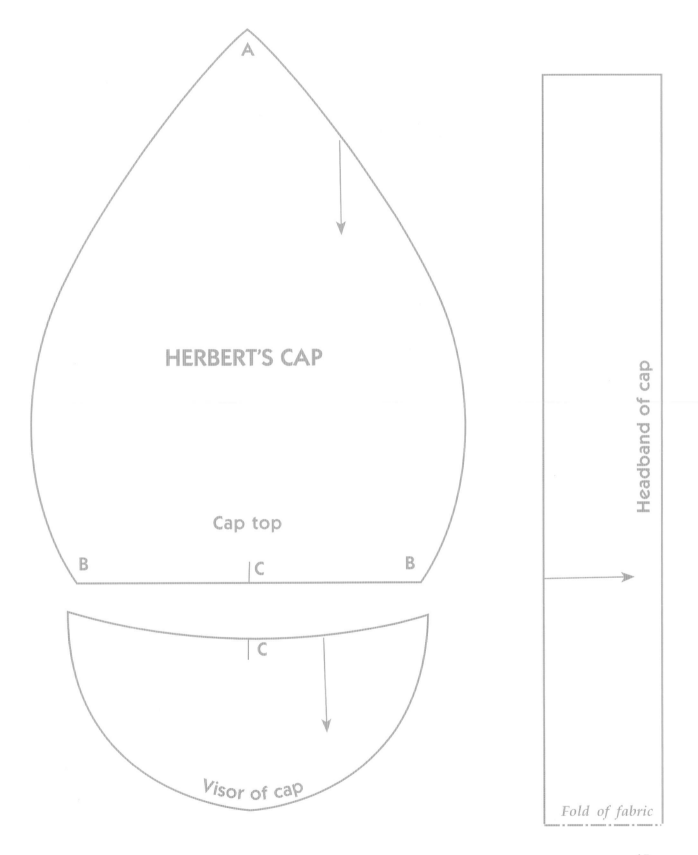

HERBERT'S CAP

Cap top

Visor of cap

Headband of cap

Fold of fabric

BENNY AND CHRISTOPHER

Benny and Christopher

are both 14 inches (35 cm) tall and are made

using the same pattern. Both are good choices to

make for small children.

Reminder: Add seam allowances around all pattern pieces when cutting. Construction is done with right sides of fabric facing, unless noted.

For Each Bear

Pattern Pieces to Cut
Front side of head: cut 2 (1 R)
Back side of head: cut 2 (1 R)
Head gusset: cut 1
Rear end: cut 1
Front of body: cut 2 (1 R)
Back of body: cut 2 (1 R)
Arm front: cut 2 (1 R)
Arm back: cut 2 (1 R)
Paw: cut 2 (1 R)
Leg: cut 4 (2 R)
Sole: cut 2 (1 R)

For Benny: cut 4 of Benny's ear (2 R)
For Christopher: cut 4 of Christopher's ear (2 R)

Sewing Instructions for a Bear
- Follow instructions in the basic techniques chapter to make the head of either bear. Insert safety eyes before stuffing the heads.
- Stitch the two front of body pieces together along the front center seamline.
- Stitch the two back of body pieces together on the back center seam-line, leaving a stuffing opening.
- Stitch the arm front to the front of body from I to K. Stitch the arm back to the back of body from G to H. Stitch the rear end to the back of body along line M–L–M.
- Pin the front and back of the body together and sew the shoulders, arm, and side seams, leaving the neck open for inserting the joint.
- For each leg: stitch two leg pieces together on the long sides from P to S and R to Q.
- Attach soles by hand, using doubled thread (see basic techniques).
- Turn legs right-side out.
- Stuff each leg to the density desired.
- Place top edges of the leg together at P to R and stitch them closed.
- Baste the leg to the front of the body, with right sides of fabric facing), aligning at P. Ease the rear end and front of the body together and stitch them from O to N to O.
- Turn body right-side out and join head to the body with the joint.
- Stuff each arm and the body.
- Embroider the nose and mouth.

MATERIALS

Christopher's Pants and Scarf

☐ 13.5 in × 29 in (35 m × .75 m) cotton fabric

☐ 16 in (.4 m) thin waistband elastic

Christopher's Shirt

☐ 10 × 35 in (.25 m × .9 m) velour

☐ 16 in (.4 m) thin elastic for the neck edge

Benny's Pajamas

☐ 18 in × 47 in (.45 m × 1.2 m) cotton fabric

☐ 3 buttons*

☐ 20 in (.5 m) white lace

☐ 1 yard (1 m) thin elastic for sleeves, neck, and pants legs

Benny's Nightcap

☐ 12 in × 16 in (.3 m × .4 m) velour

☐ 1 little bell*

*Omit buttons and bell if bear is for a small child.

Christopher's Pants

Before you cut fabric: Join Christopher's pants pattern part 1 to part 2 along line A–B.

Pants Pieces to Cut

Pants: cut 2 (1 R)

Sewing the Pants

• Stitch the pants pieces together at the front and back center seams. Sew the leg inseams closed.

• Turn under the elastic casing at the foldline and stitch, leaving a small opening for the elastic, and insert it. Hem the pants legs.

Christopher's Shirt

Shirt Pieces to Cut

Combined front and back of shirt piece: cut 2 on folded fabric
Sleeve: cut 2 on folded fabric

Sewing Christopher's Shirt

• Stitch each arm to the shirt front and back from G to H. Stitch the underarm and side seams. Turn the shirt right-side out.

• Turn the self-facing at the neck inside and stitch along the seamline, leaving a small opening to insert the elastic for gathering the neckline, and insert it. Hem sleeves and lower edge of shirt.

Benny's Pajamas

Before you cut fabric: Join pajama body pattern part 1 and pajama body part 2 along line C–D. The same pattern is used for the front and back.

Pajama Pieces to Cut

Pajama body: cut 2 on folded fabric
Sleeves: cut 2 on folded fabric

Sewing Benny's Pajamas

• Stitch each sleeve to the front and back of the pajama body from I to K. Stitch the sleeve inseams closed. Stitch the front and back pajama body together at the sides and around the leg inseams.

• Fold in and stitch the self-facing around the neck edge, but leave a small opening and insert the elastic to gather the neck opening. Sew buttons on front.

• Turn under seam allowances at the sleeve and the leg openings; leave a small space to insert the thin elastic; insert it and gather to correct size for bear.

• Hem the lace at each short end; turn under one long edge and run some embroidery thread through; pull it to gather around the bear's neck.

Benny's Nightcap

Before you cut fabric: Join nightcap pattern parts 1 and 2 at line E–F.

Nightcap Pieces to Cut

Nightcap: cut 2 (1 R)
Strip for edge: cut bias strip about 16 in (40 cm) long from pajama fabric

Sewing Benny's Nightcap

• Put the two nightcap pieces together and stitch around the curved edges. Sew on the bias strip at the head edge to finish.

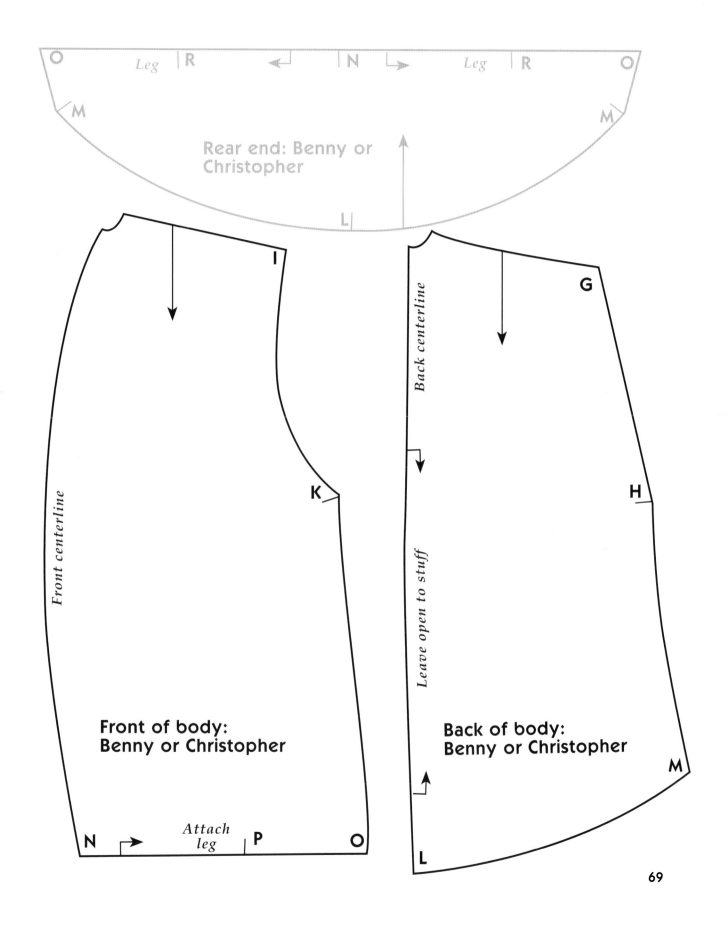

Rear end: Benny or Christopher

Front centerline

I

K

**Front of body:
Benny or Christopher**

N → *Attach leg* P O

Back centerline

Leave open to stuff

G

H

**Back of body:
Benny or Christopher**

M

L

69

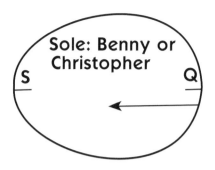

Sole: Benny or Christopher

S   Q

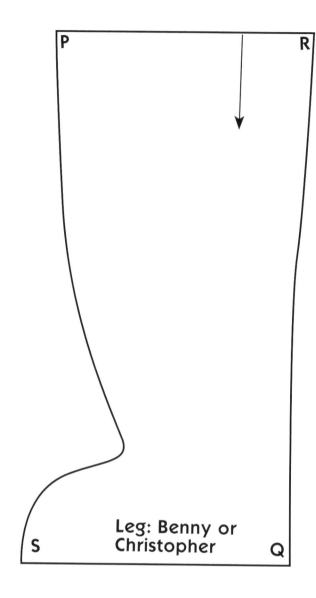

P   R

Leg: Benny or
Christopher

S   Q

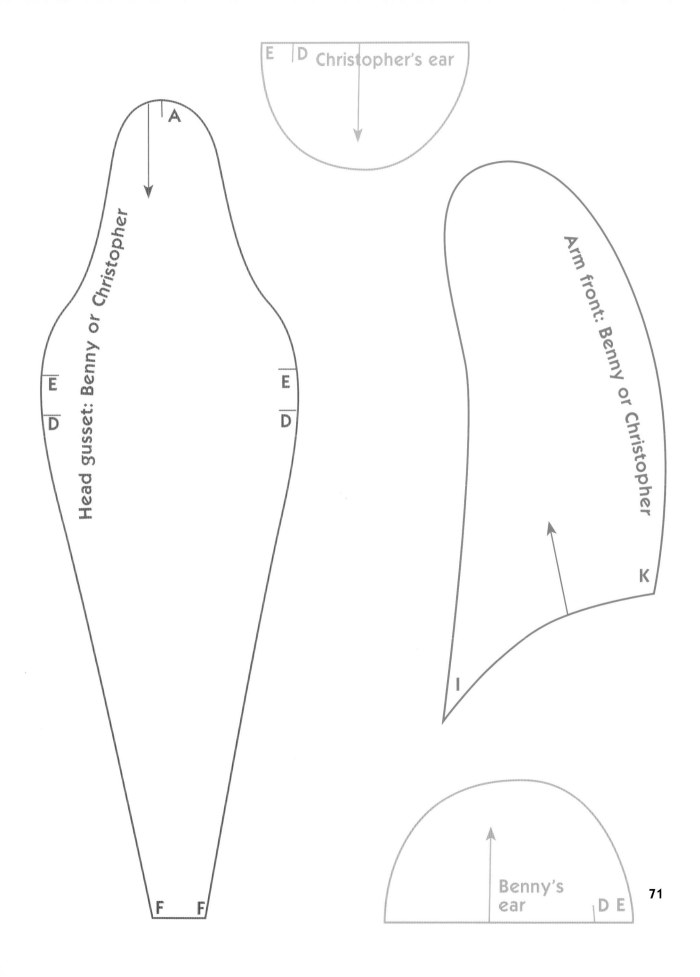

E D Christopher's ear

A

Head gusset: Benny or Christopher

E

E

D

D

Arm front: Benny or Christopher

K

I

Benny's
ear

D E

F F

71

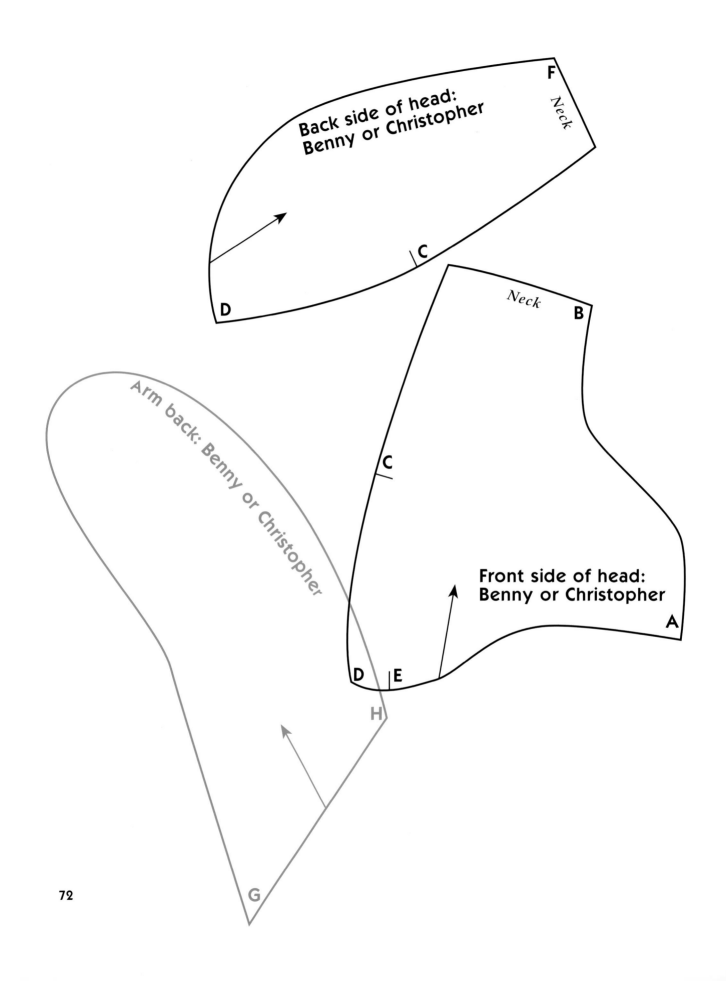

Back side of head:
Benny or Christopher

F

Neck

C

D

Neck

B

C

Front side of head:
Benny or Christopher

A

D E

Arm back: Benny or Christopher

H

G

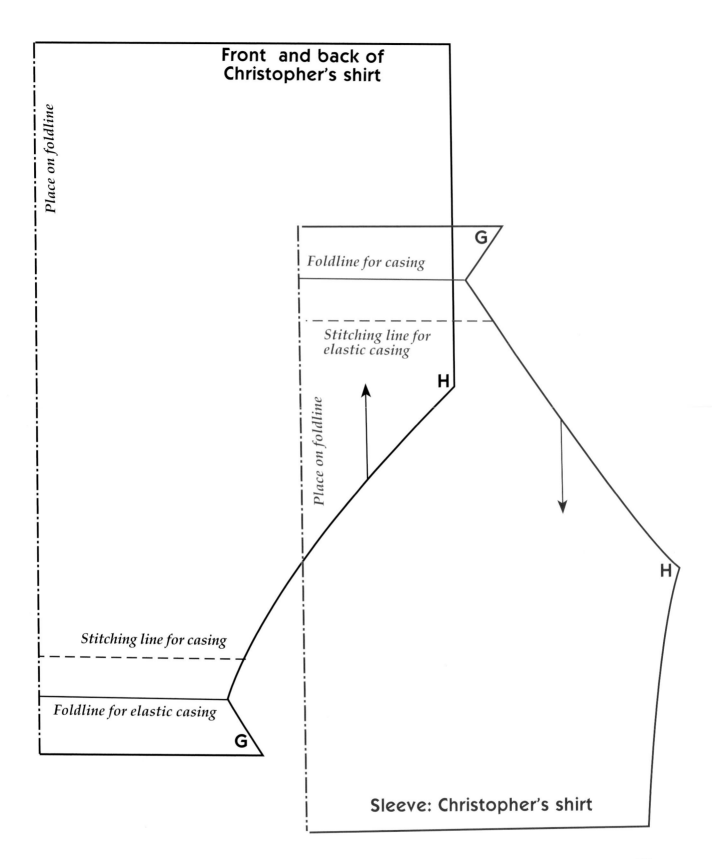

Front and back of Christopher's shirt

Place on foldline

Foldline for casing

G

Stitching line for elastic casing

Place on foldline

H

H

Stitching line for casing

Foldline for elastic casing

G

Sleeve: Christopher's shirt

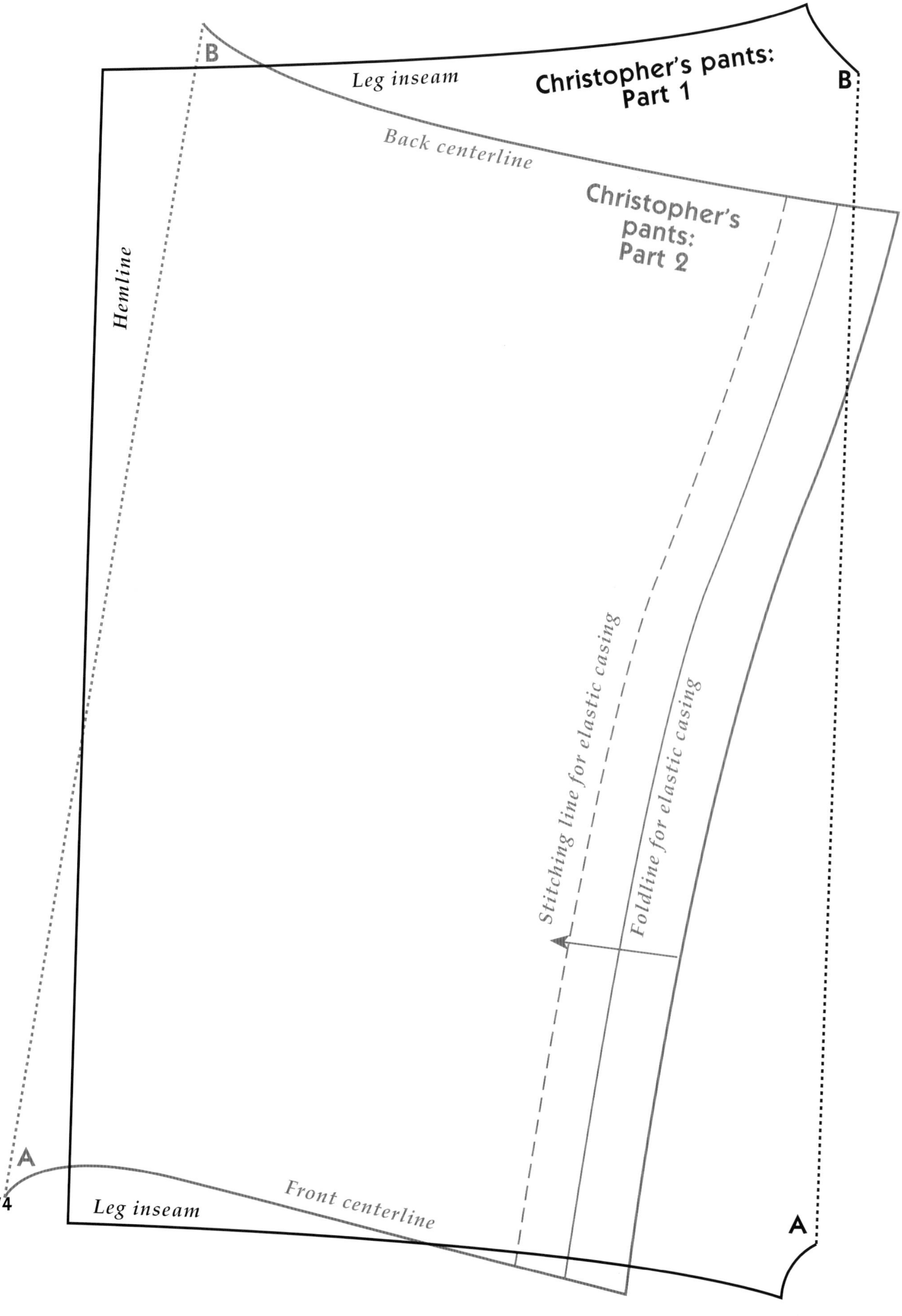

B

Leg inseam

**Christopher's pants:
Part 1**

B

Back centerline

**Christopher's
pants:
Part 2**

Hemline

Stitching line for elastic casing

Foldline for elastic casing

A

74

Leg inseam

Front centerline

A

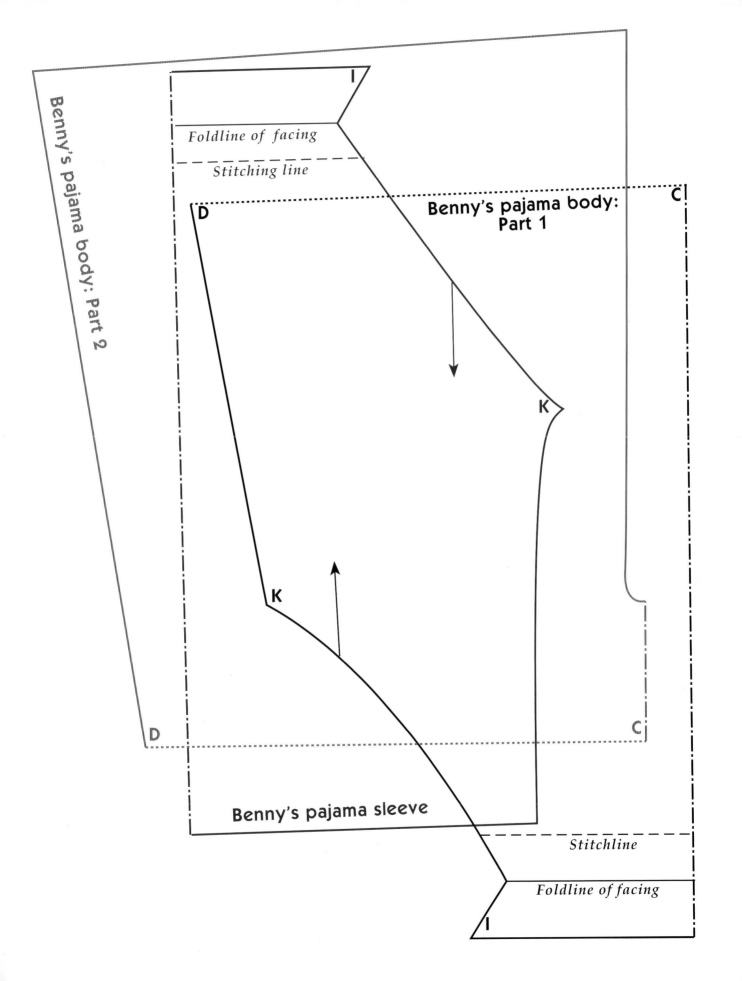

Benny's pajama body: Part 2

I

Foldline of facing

Stitching line

D

Benny's pajama body:
Part 1

C

K

K

D

C

Benny's pajama sleeve

Stitchline

Foldline of facing

I

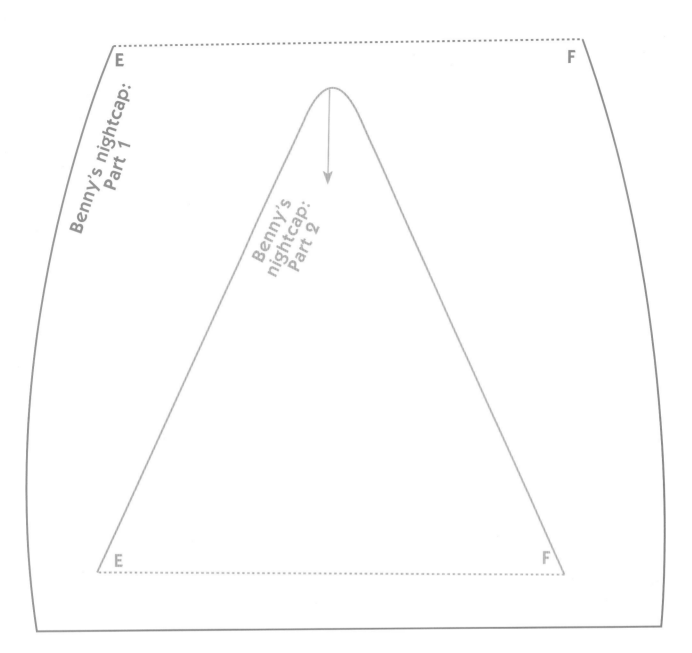

Benny's nightcap.
Part 1

Benny's nightcap.
Part 2

E

F

E

F

BARTLEBY

Bartleby

is 14 inches (35 cm) tall. His paws and soles are made from the same fabric as his body. Make him a leather vest and a pair of pants in a complementary color. Then he will be ready for a hike in the woods— all that he needs is his walking stick. . . .

Reminder: Add seam allowances around the pattern pieces when cutting. All construction is done with right sides of fabric facing, unless noted.

The Bear

Bartleby: Pieces to Cut
Side of head: cut 2 (1 R)
Head gusset: cut 1
Ear: cut 4 (2 R)
Front of body: cut 2 (1 R)
Back of body: cut 2 (1 R)
Arm: cut 2 (1 R)
Paw: cut 2 (1 R)
Inner leg: cut 2 (1 R)
Outer leg: cut 2 (1 R)
Sole: cut 2

Sewing Instructions for Bear
Follow the instructions given in the basic techniques chapter, but make the arms as described in the instructions for Scotty (page 122).

MATERIALS

Bartleby's Shirt
- 8 in × 43 in (.2 m × 1.1 m) lightweight striped cotton batiste or old man's shirt
- matching folded bias binding
- 3 shirt buttons
- sewing thread

Bartleby's Pants
- 8 in × 31 in (.2 m × .8 m) narrow-wale gray corduroy
- red sewing thread
- ¼ in (.6 cm) waistband elastic
- 2 pieces of leather 3.5 in × ¼ in (9 cm × .5 cm) from vest scraps

Bartleby's Vest
- red or brown leather remnant 18 in × 6.25 in (.45 m × .16 m); take pattern with you when you buy it
- sewing thread
- needle for sewing leather, or leather glue

Bartleby's Shirt

Shirt Pieces to Cut
Back of shirt: cut 1 on folded fabric
Front of shirt: cut 2 (1 R)
Sleeve: cut 2

Sewing Instructions for Shirt
- Stitch front and back together at the shoulder seams.
- Slightly gather the sleeves where marked and then sew sleeves into armholes.
- Hem sleeves.
- Turn and stitch the self-facing of the shirt front under along the foldline; press and stitch in place.
- Make three buttonholes on the right front.
- Hem the shirt's lower edge.
- Finish the neck edge with bias binding.
- Sew on the buttons.

Bartleby's Pants

Pants Pieces to Cut
Front: cut 2 (1 R)
Back: cut 2 (1 R)
Pocket: cut 2 (1 R)

Sewing the Pants
- With red thread, hem the angled edges of the pockets by folding the seam allowance inside and press; baste and then stitch the pockets to the pants front.
- Stitch the front pieces together along the center seamline; stitch the pleats (C–C; D–D; E–E).
- Stitch the back pieces together along the center seamline. Pin the front and back together, and stitch the side seams and the leg inseam.
- Turn the elastic casing at the waist inside on the foldline and stitch on the stitching line; leaving a ½ inch (1 cm) opening to insert for the elastic.
- Measure the bear's waist and insert correct length of elastic. Stitch the opening closed.
- Hem the pants legs; attach a small leather strip to each pleat and tie into a knot.

Bartleby's Vest

Cutting and Sewing
Before you cut leather: Cut the vest pattern on folded tracing paper. Open out and paste on template cardboard. Do not add seam allowances if you use leather, except along line A–B.

Place the pattern template on the wrong side of the leather; outline with a pencil or grease pencil. Cut out of the leather. The vest now consists of one piece of leather; all you have to do is sew (or glue) the shoulder seams. Match along line A–B and sew or glue.

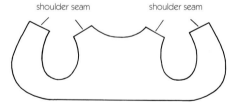

78

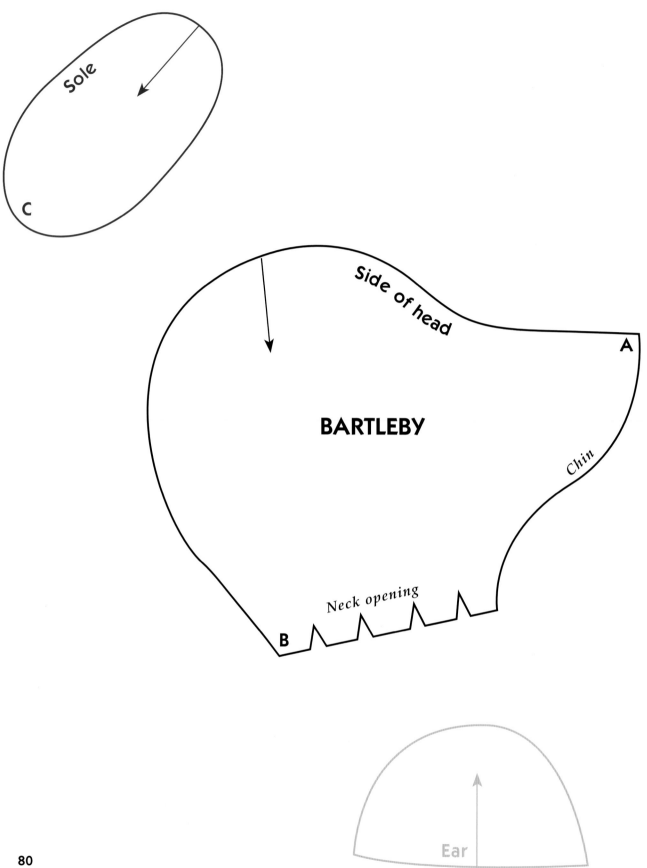

Sole

C

Side of head

A

BARTLEBY

Chin

Neck opening

B

Ear

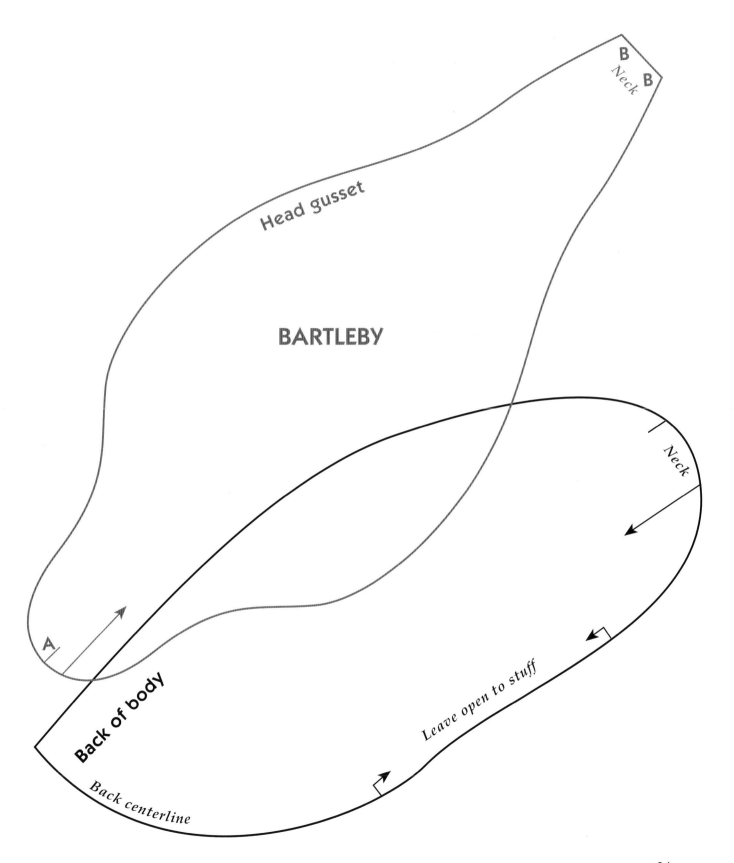

Head gusset

BARTLEBY

B

B

Neck

Neck

A

Back of body

Leave open to stuff

Back centerline

81

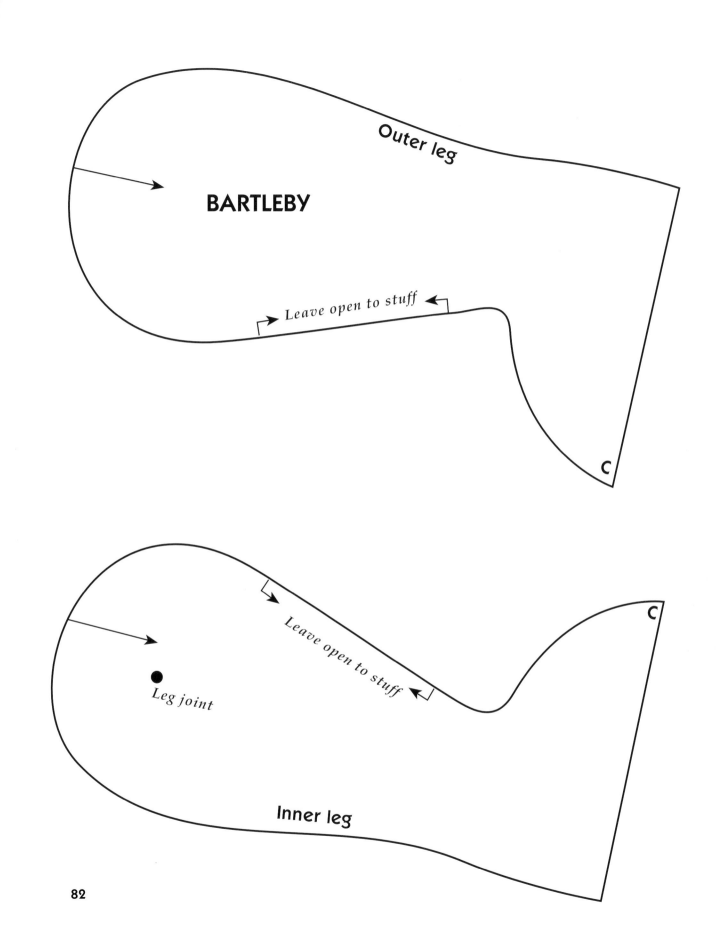

BARTLEBY

Outer leg

Leave open to stuff

C

Leave open to stuff

C

Leg joint

Inner leg

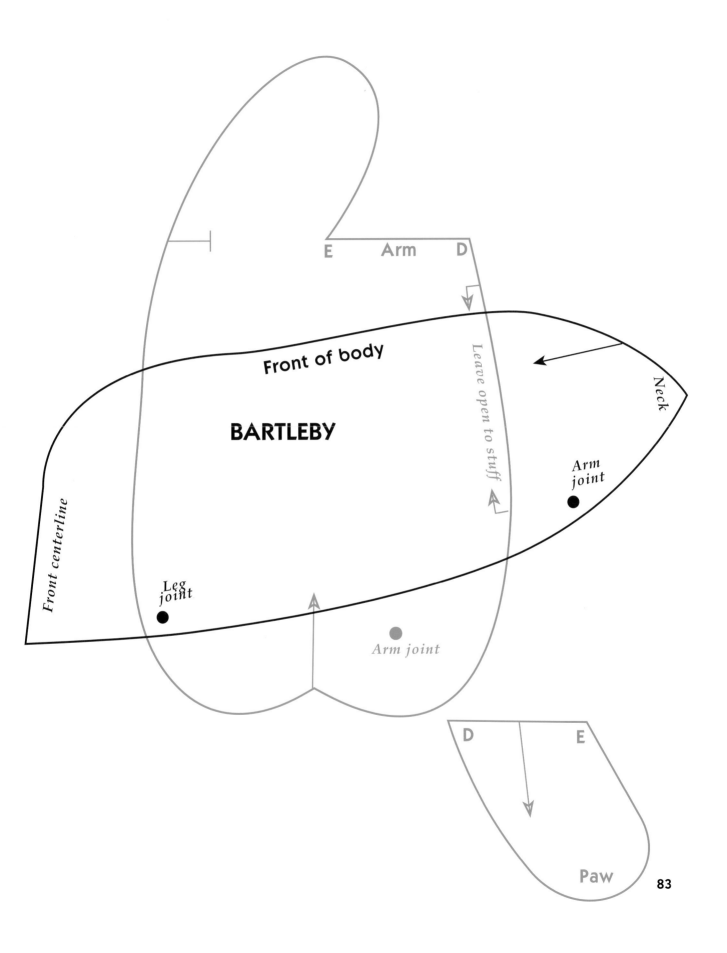

E   Arm   D

Front of body

BARTLEBY

Leave open to stuff

Neck

Front centerline

Arm joint

Leg joint

Arm joint

D   E

Paw

83

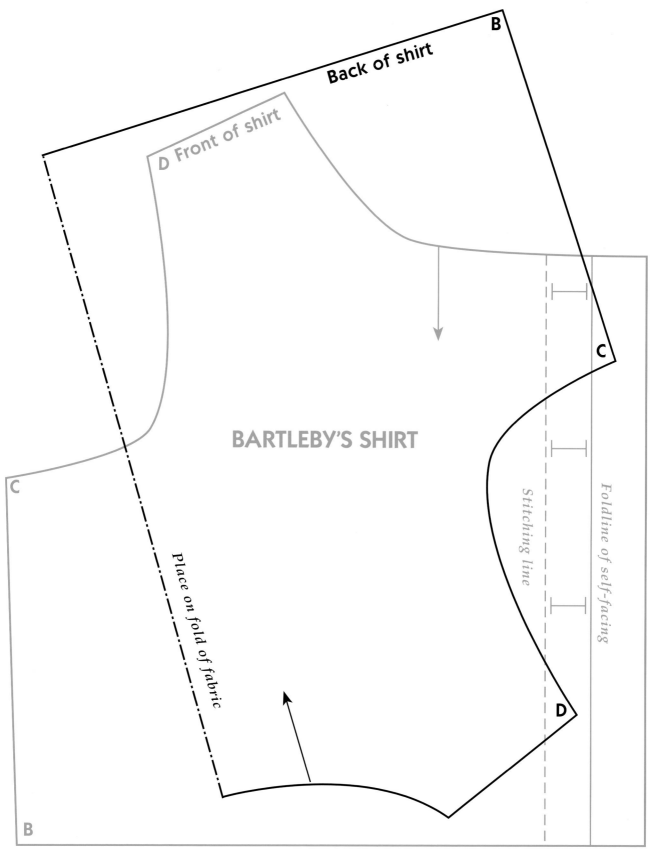

B

Back of shirt

D Front of shirt

C

BARTLEBY'S SHIRT

Place on fold of fabric

Stitching line

Foldline of self-facing

C

D

B

84

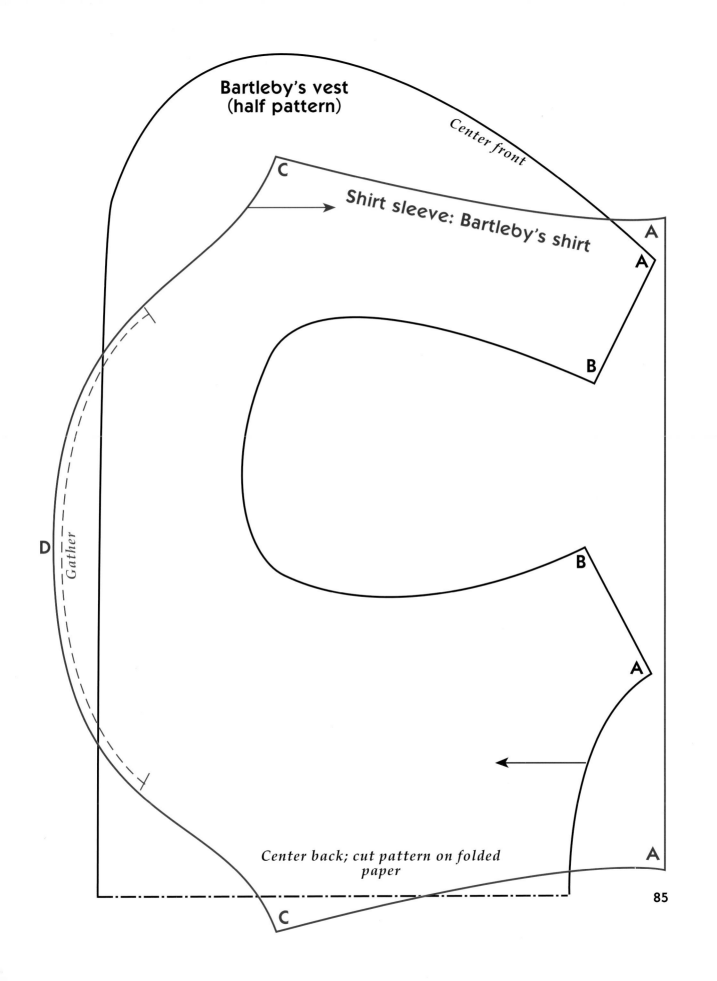

Bartleby's vest
(half pattern)

Center front

C

Shirt sleeve: Bartleby's shirt

A
A

B

D

Gather

B

A

A

Center back; cut pattern on folded paper

C

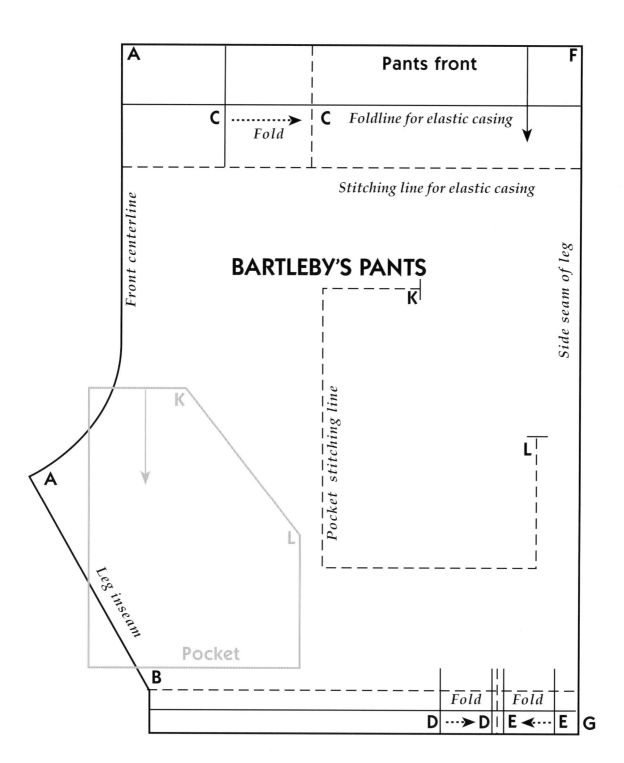

BARTLEBY'S PANTS

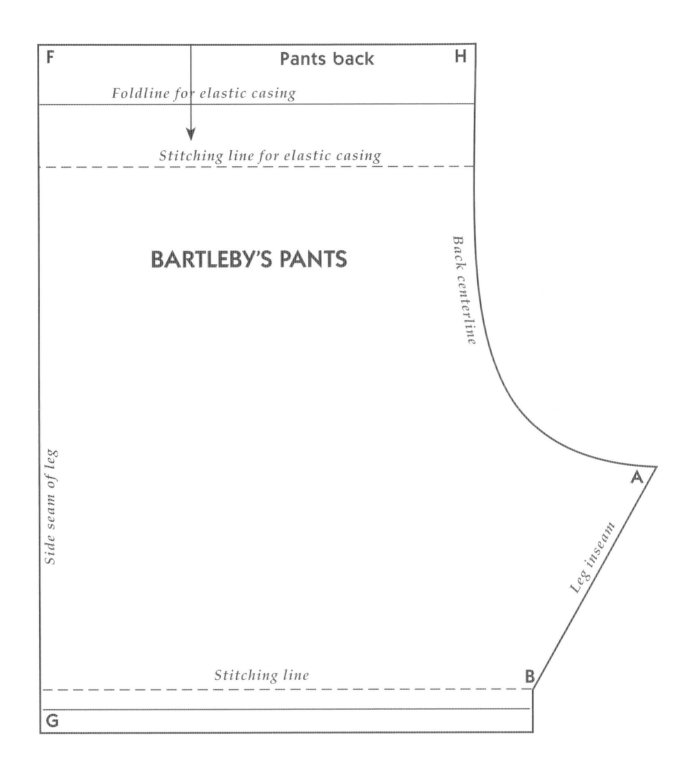

F

Pants back

H

Foldline for elastic casing

Stitching line for elastic casing

BARTLEBY'S PANTS

Back centerline

A

Side seam of leg

Leg inseam

Stitching line

B

G

PETE

Pete

a cool blond bear, is 16 inches tall (40 cm) and has thin fur. If you use a thick, long-haired mohair fur fabric and knit him a thick sweater, he will look entirely different.

Reminder: Add seam allowances around the pattern pieces when cutting. Construction is done with right sides of fabric facing, unless noted.

The Bear

Before you cut fabric: Trace the leg pattern on folded tracing paper. Open out the pattern; transfer marks to both halves. Make a cardboard template of the whole leg pattern.

Pete: Pieces to Cut

Side of head: cut 2 (1 R)
Head gusset: cut 1
Ears: cut 4 (2 R)
Body: cut 2 (1 R)
Outer arm: cut 2 (1 R)
Inner arm: cut 2 (1 R)
Paw: cut 2 (1 R)*
Leg: cut 2 (1 R)
Sole: cut 2 (1 R)*

*Cut Pete's paws and soles one at a time from leather.

Sewing Instructions for Bear

Make Pete according to instructions in the basic techniques chapter. With a leather-sewing needle, sew on paws and soles by machine or by hand.

Pants

Pants Pieces to Cut

Pants: cut 2 on folded fabric

Sewing the Pants

- Place both pants pieces together and stitch the center seams together in front and in back.
- Turn the self-facing at the waistline to the wrong side and stitch along the stitching line, leaving a ½ inch (1 cm) opening to insert the elastic.
- Stitch the inseams; hem the legs.
- Measure the bear's waist; cut and insert the elastic; close opening.

Fisherman's Shirt

Shirt Pieces to Cut

Shirt back: cut 1 on folded fabric
Shirt front: cut 1 on folded fabric
Sleeve: cut 2 on folded fabric
Pocket: cut 1
Stand-up collar: cut strip 10 in × 2 in (26 cm × 4 cm)
Facing: cut 1 on folded fabric

Sewing the Shirt

- Place facing on the shirt front with right sides of fabric face to face. Stitch facing to front on both sides of the slit marking, ⅛ inch (3 mm) from the marking, down to E. Carefully cut the slit open. Turn facing inside; stitch close to edge.
- Hem pocket's top edge; press seam allowances of other edges inside. Sew pocket on shirt front below the slit.
- Stitch the shirt front and back together at the shoulder seams, from A to B. Sew on sleeves. Stitch sleeve seams and shirt sides.
- Use the strip of fabric to make the stand-up collar; sew it to the neck opening. Hem sleeves and shirt.

MATERIALS

For the Bear

- 21 in × 54 in (.3 m × 1.4 m) yellow mohair fur fabric
- pair of glass eyes, 16 mm size
- joint set for an 18 in tall (45 cm) bear
- 29 oz (800 g) stuffing
- leather remnants for paws and soles
- sewing thread
- needle for sewing leather
- strong thread
- black pearl embroidery thread

Pete's Shirt and Pants

- 39 in × 10 in (1 m × .25 m) blue-and-white striped cotton fabric
- 27 in × 21 in (.7 m × .3 m) thin blue fabric or denim
- small red kerchief
- thin waistband elastic
- blue sewing thread

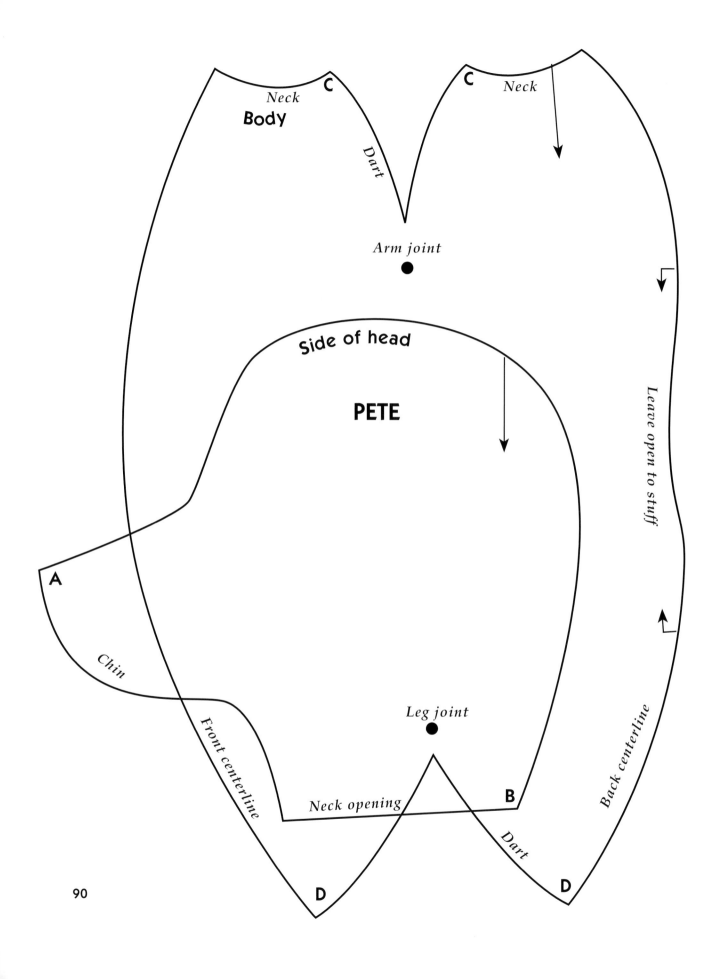

Neck

Body

C

Dart

C

Neck

Arm joint

Side of head

PETE

Leave open to stuff

A

Chin

Leg joint

Front centerline

Back centerline

Neck opening

B

Dart

D

D

90

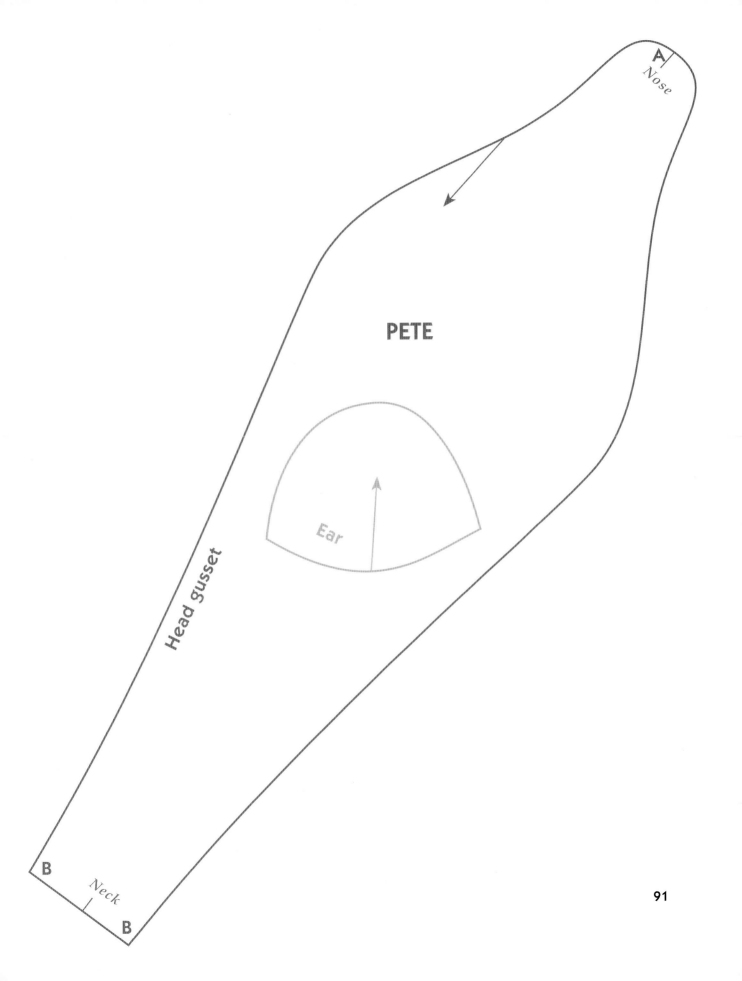

A

Nose

PETE

Ear

Head gusset

B

Neck

B

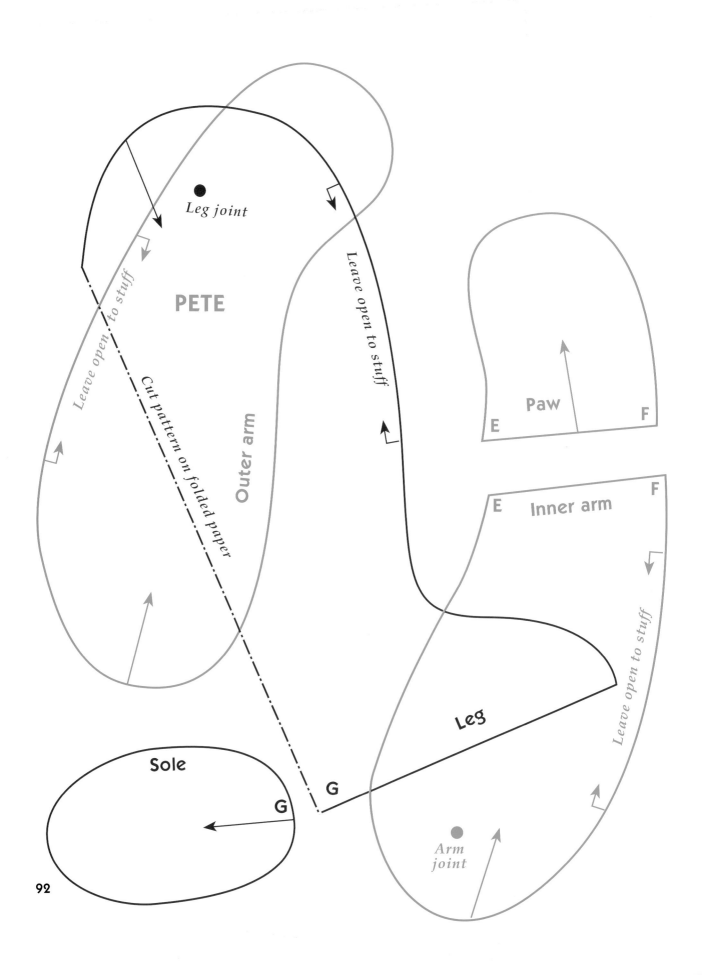

Leg joint

PETE

Leave open to stuff

Cut pattern on folded paper

Outer arm

Leave open to stuff

Paw

E   F

E   Inner arm   F

Leave open to stuff

Leg

Sole

G

G

Arm joint

92

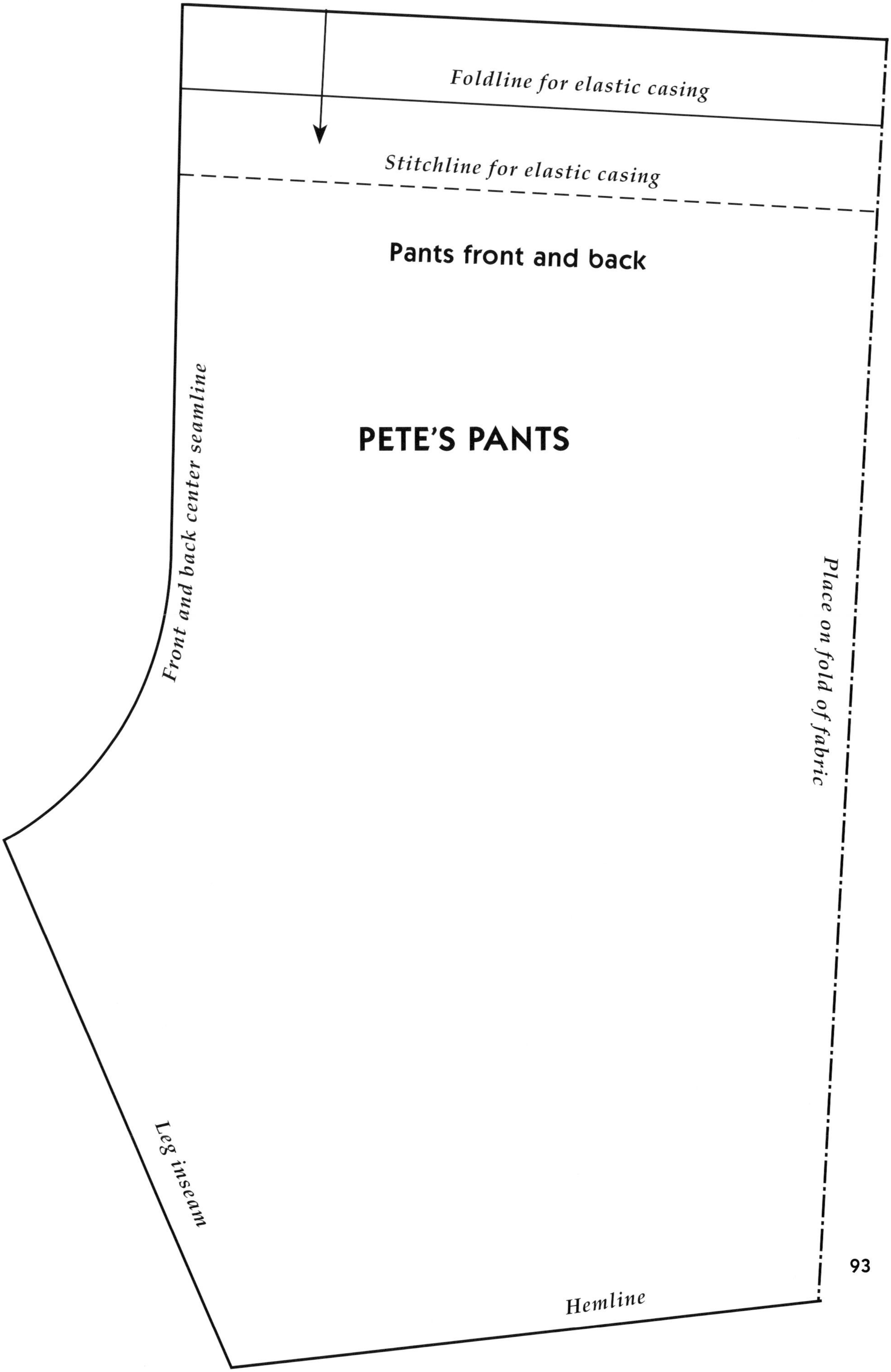

Foldline for elastic casing

Stitchline for elastic casing

Pants front and back

PETE'S PANTS

Front and back center seamline

Place on fold of fabric

Leg inseam

93

Hemline

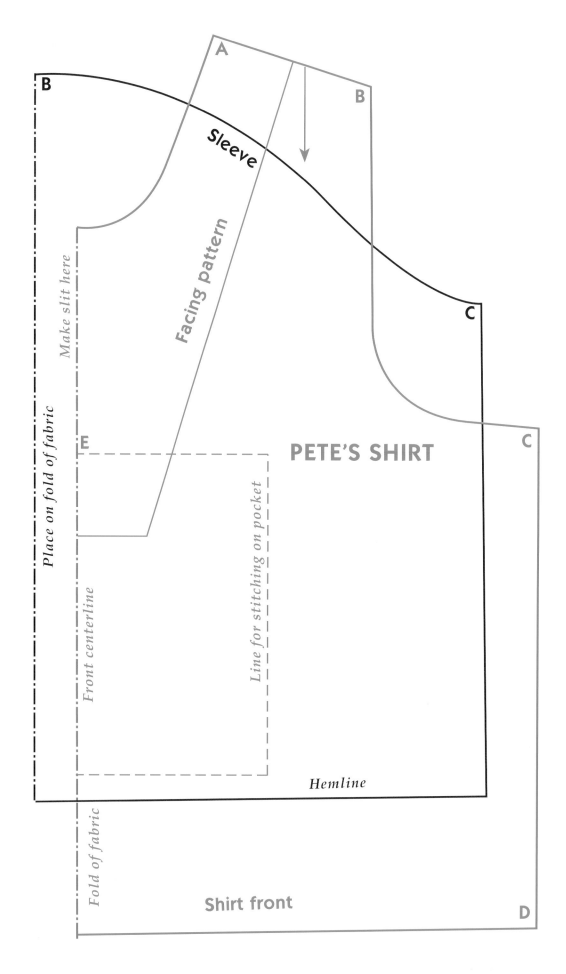

A

B

B

Sleeve

C

Facing pattern

C

Make slit here

Place on fold of fabric

PETE'S SHIRT

E

Front centerline

Line for stitching on pocket

Hemline

Fold of fabric

94

Shirt front

D

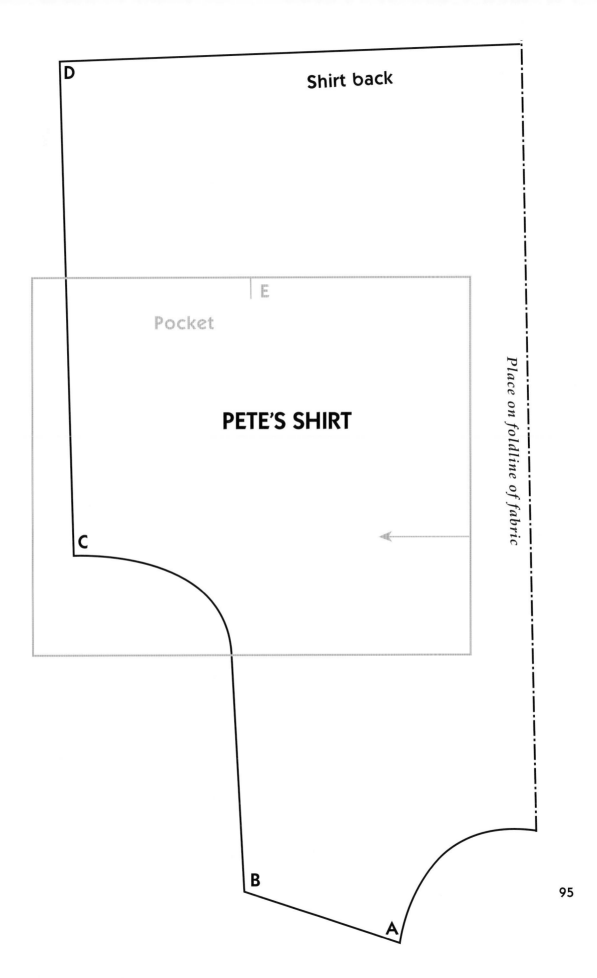

Shirt back

D

E

Pocket

PETE'S SHIRT

Place on foldline of fabric

C

B

A

95

RALPH

Ralph

is 15 inches tall (38 cm) and a rather
muscular little fellow. No wonder,
considering his training. If you want
to use long-haired fur fabric for a
small bear, reduce the seam allowance
near the arm and leg joints a bit.

Reminder: Add seam allowances
around the pattern pieces when cutting. All construction is done with
right sides of fabric facing, unless
noted.

The Bear

Ralph: Pieces to Cut
Side of head: cut 2 (1 R)
Head gusset: cut 1
Ears: cut 4 (2 R)
Body: cut 2 (1 R)
Inner arm: cut 2 (1 R)
Outer arm: cut 2 (1 R)
Inner leg: cut 2 (1 R)
Outer leg: cut 2 (1 R)
Sole: cut 2

Sewing Instructions for Bear
Sew Ralph according to the instructions given in the chapter on basic
techniques.

The Bodysuit

Bodysuit Pieces to Cut
Cut 2 of the bodysuit pattern on folded fabric.

Sewing the Bodysuit
• Stitch the bodysuit pieces together
  at shoulders, side seams, and inner
  leg seams. Turn under and sew the
  seam allowance at the armholes,
  leg edges, and neck edge.

MATERIALS
For the Bear
☐ 20 in × 54 in (.5 m × 1.4 m) beige antique-look cotton plush
☐ pair of black glass eyes, 14 mm size
☐ joint set for an 18-inch tall (45 cm) bear
☐ 22 oz (600 g) stuffing
☐ sewing thread to match fur
☐ black embroidery thread
☐ strong thread
Bodysuit
☐ 24 in × 10 in (.6 m × .25 m) striped jersey or an old T-shirt
☐ matching sewing thread

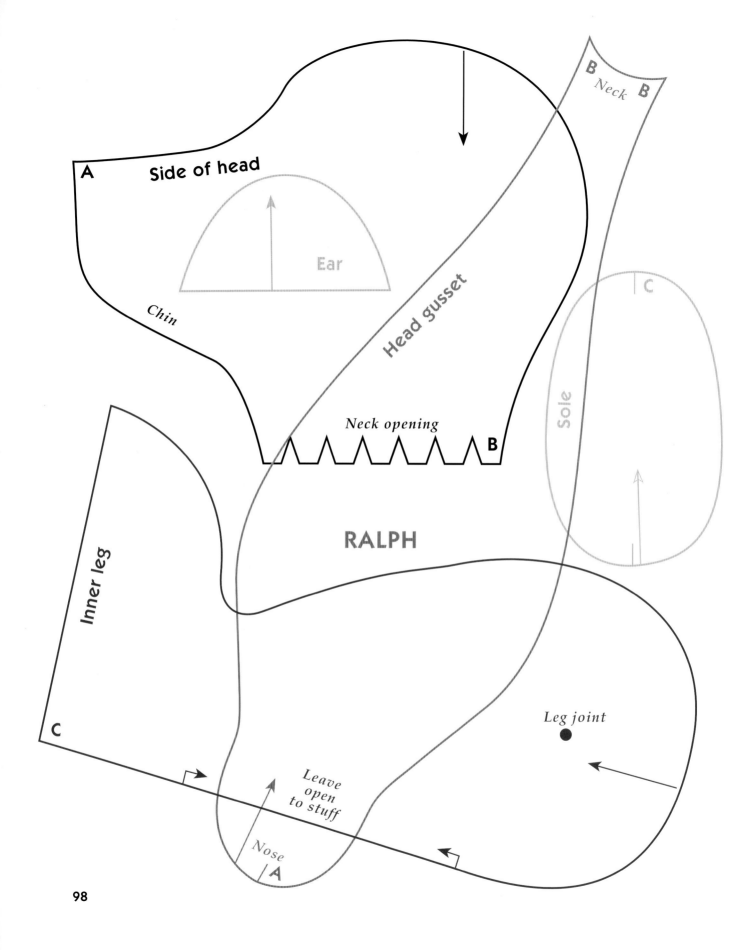

A

Side of head

Ear

Chin

Head gusset

B

B
Neck

C

Sole

Neck opening

B

RALPH

Inner leg

C

Leg joint

Leave
open
to stuff

Nose

A

98

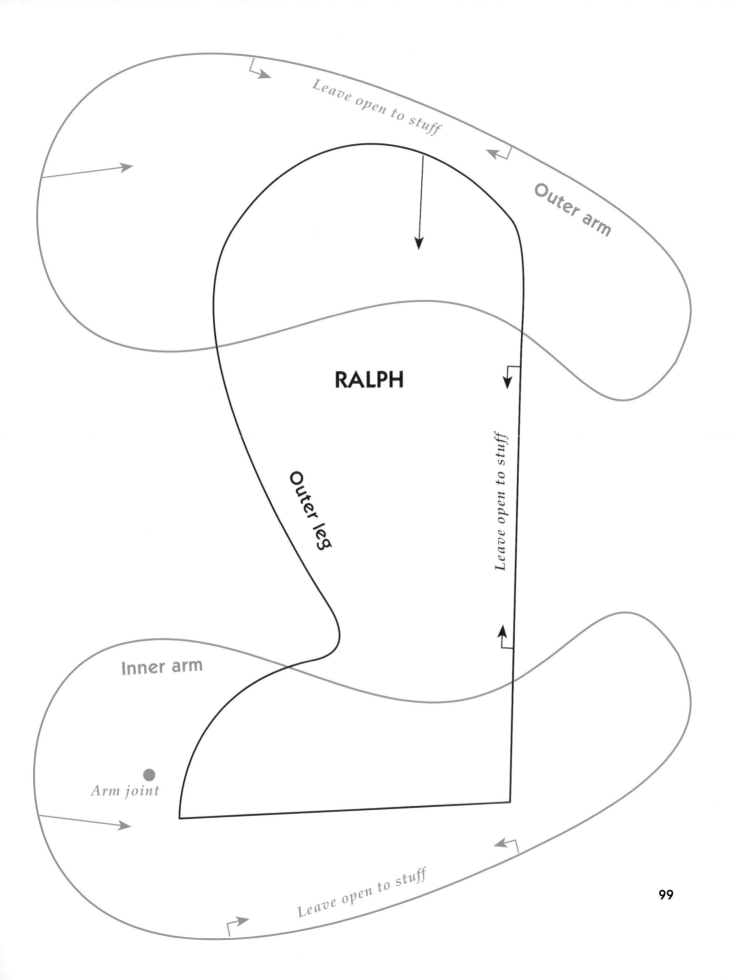

Leave open to stuff

Outer arm

RALPH

Outer leg

Leave open to stuff

Inner arm

Arm joint

Leave open to stuff

99

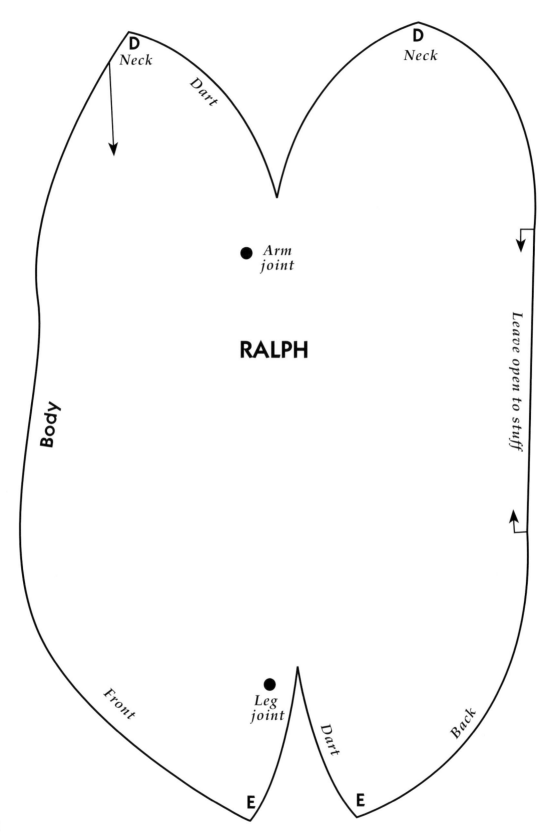

D

Neck

Dart

D

Neck

● Arm joint

RALPH

Body

Leave open to stuff

Front

● Leg joint

Dart

Back

E

E

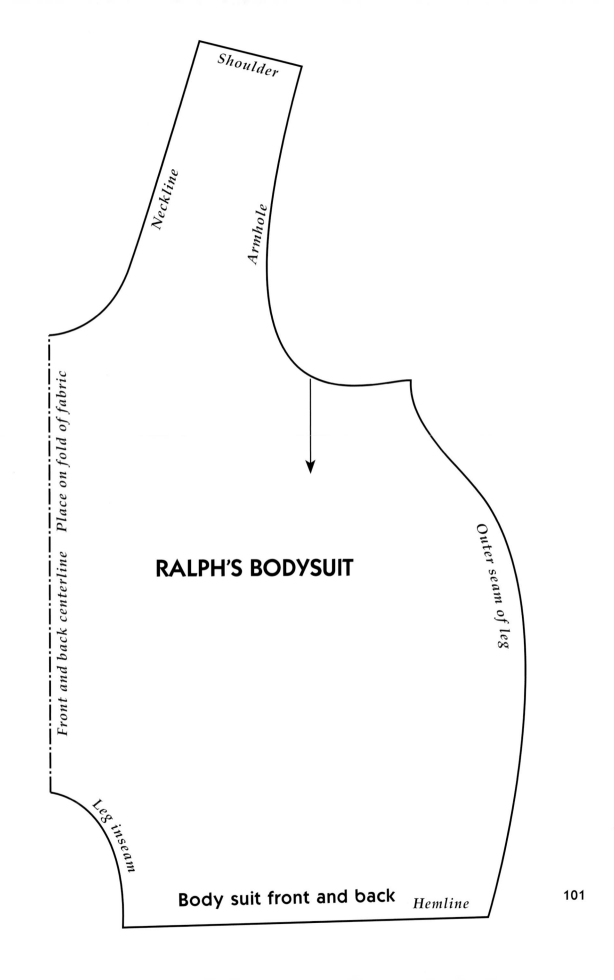

Shoulder

Neckline

Armhole

Place on fold of fabric

Front and back centerline

Outer seam of leg

RALPH'S BODYSUIT

Leg inseam

Body suit front and back Hemline

101

MATERIALS FOR
A BEAR

- 16 in × 54 in (.4 m × 1.4 m) gray or cinnamon-colored mohair fur fabric
- pair of black glass eyes, 10 mm size
- cotter-pin joint set for a 16 inch tall (40 cm) bear
- about 18 oz (500 g) stuffing granules
- 300 g polyester stuffing
- sewing thread to match fur
- strong thread
- black embroidery thread

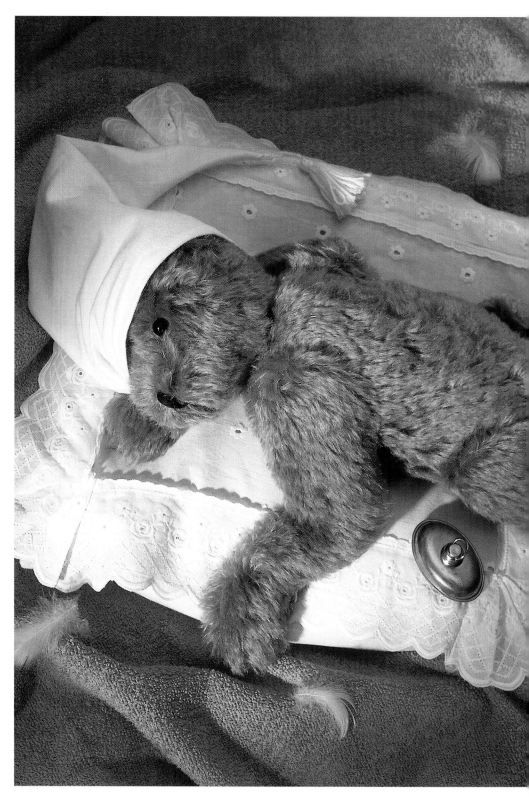

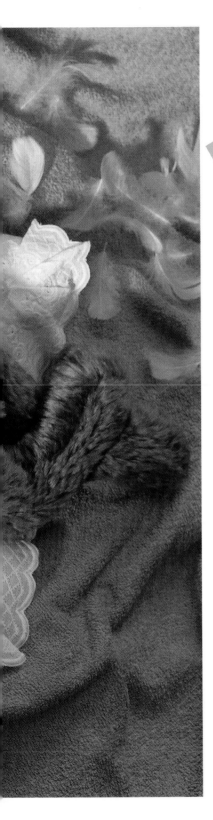

PEARL AND GOLDIE

Pearl and Goldie

are both 15 inches tall (38 cm) and
are made using the same pattern, but
with different arms, legs, soles, and
ears.

Reminder: Add seam allowances
around the pattern pieces when cutting. All construction is done with
right sides of fabric facing, unless
noted.

The Bears

Pearl: Pattern Pieces to Cut
Side of head: cut 2 (1 R)
Head gusset: cut 1
Pearl's ear: cut 4 (2 R)
Front of body, Pearl: cut 2 (1R)
Back of body, Pearl: cut 2 (1 R)
Pearl's leg: cut 4 (2 R)
Pearl's arm: cut 4 (2 R)
Pearl's sole: cut 2 (1 R)

Goldie: Pattern Pieces to Cut
Side of head: cut 2 (1 R)
Head gusset: cut 1
Goldie's ear: cut 4 (2 R)
Front of body, Goldie: cut 2 (1 R)
Back of body, Goldie: cut 2 (1 R)
Inner leg, Goldie: cut 2 (1 R)
Outer leg, Goldie: cut 2 (1 R)
Goldie's sole: cut 2 (1 R)
Inner arm, Goldie: cut 2 (1 R)
Outer arm, Goldie: cut 2 (1 R)

Sewing Instructions for Goldie
Goldie (small photo on the left) is
made according to the instructions
described in the chapter on basic
techniques.

Sewing Instructions for Pearl
Pearl (large photo) is made a bit differently than Goldie.

- Sew the arms and legs without
  leaving openings for stuffing, but
  leave a stuffing hole when you sew
  the body pieces together, as usual.
  Take one arm (still inside out) and
  the joint mechanism for that arm;
  place the joint disk on the inner
  arm close to the seam at the top.
  Make sure that the distances on the
  right and left of the disk are equal.
  Mark a vertical line for a slit to
  insert the joint mechanism starting
  at the lower edge of the disk and
  going up almost to the top seam.

- With a pair of nail scissors, cut
  straight up along the line, almost to
  the top seam. Turn the arm right-
  side out through the opening.

- Stuff a little polyester stuffing into
  the paws and fill the rest of the
  limb loosely with granules.

- When you have stuffed up to the
  joint area, insert stuffing in the top
  (shoulder area) of the arm. Take
  the joint mechanism for that arm.
  First put the metal washer on the
  cotter pin and then the disk.* Insert
  the disk with the pin through the
  slit into the arm.

- Push the joint mechanism (disk,
  washer and cotter pin) up until it
  touches the top seam.

*If you are using screw joints, you can
glue the head of the bolt to the washer
and disk with epoxy before inserting
them.

- Close the slit by hand with small stitches, leaving the cotter pin sticking out.
- Do the other arm in the same way. The legs are done in the same manner.
- Attach arms and legs to the body in the usual way. (If you used screw joints, you can tighten the nuts using a ratchet wrench.)
- Stuff the head firmly with polyester and attach to the body. Add a little stuffing to the belly and between the legs. Fill the rest of the body with granules.
- Stuff the shoulder and neck area loosely with the stuffing material in order to stabilize the head. Stitch the opening in the back of the body closed.
- See the chapter on basic techniques for instructions on attaching the eyes and embroidering the nose.

Pearl's Nightcap

Before you cut fabric: Join part 1 and part 2 of Pearl's nightcap pattern along line A–B to make the complete nightcap pattern.

Nightcap Pieces to Cut
Cut 1 nightcap pattern on folded fabric

Sewing the Nightcap
- With the fabric still folded right sides together, stitch the curved edges of the nightcap piece together.
- Hem the straight edge.
- Turn the nightcap right-side out. Make a pompom from cotton yarn and sew to the tip of the nightcap.

Goldie's Dress

Dress Pieces to Cut
Dress front and back: cut 2 on folded fabric
Yoke front: cut 2 on folded fabric
Yoke back: cut 2 on folded fabric

Sewing Goldie's Dress
- Gather the dress front and back pieces at the upper edge, as indicated on the pattern, to 3½ inches (9 cm).
- Put the dress front and back pieces together and sew the side seams.
- Finish the armholes with bias binding.
- Hem the dress and sew on lace at the bottom.
- Reinforce one each of the front and back yoke pieces with interfacing on the wrong side of the fabric.
- Take one piece of lace 18 in (45 cm) long lace and gather to fit the lower edge of the yoke front. Repeat for the yoke back. Stitch the lace to the right side of the yoke front with raw edges of lace and yoke aligned. Repeat for the yoke back.
- Take a second yoke front and put it over the yoke front with the lace stitched on with right sides facing. Stitch the two yoke front pieces together along all sides except in the front from A to A.
- Repeat the previous step for the yoke back.
- Trim the seam allowances at the points, clip the curves, and turn the yoke pieces right-side out. Press.
- Baste the gathered dress top inside the yoke openings, front and back. Turn under the yoke and lace seam allowances, and stitch the yoke to the dress, close to the edge.

- Make buttonholes and sew on buttons at the shoulders as indicated on the yoke patterns.

Goldie's Pants

Before you cut fabric: The pants pattern is given in 4 parts.
- Join pants pattern part 1 to pants pattern part 3 from A to E.
- Join pants pattern part 2 to pants pattern part 1 from E to D.
- Join pants pattern part 4 to pants pattern part 2 at E–B and to pants pattern part 3 at E–C to make the assembled pants pattern.

Pants Pattern Pieces to Cut
Assembled pants pattern: cut 2 (1 R)

Sewing the Pants
- Stitch the two pants pieces together, joining the front center seam to front center seam and back center seam to back center seam.
- Stitch the inseams of each pants leg closed.
- Hem the pants legs, but leave an opening for the elastic, and insert it. Close the opening.
- Stitch down the seam allowance at the waistline but leave an opening for the elastic, and insert it. Close the opening.

Goldie's Collar
- Gather the lace to fit the bear's neck.
- Stitch the lace to the center of the ribbon, with the edges of the ribbon covering the raw edges of the lace.

Goldie's Shoes

Shoe Pieces to Cut*
Upper shoe: cut 2 (1 R)
Lower shoe: cut 2 (1 R)

*Add seam allowances to the shoe pieces only along the back centerline.

Sewing the Shoes
- Fold the shoe bottom in half with right sides together and stitch up the center back seam. Turn the shoe right-side out. Fold the back seam down over the curved part of the shoe bottom so the F of the center back seam lines up with the F of the heel. Stitch across the heel slit with overcast stitches.
- Gather the shoe bottom along the gathering line that is centered at G.
- Pin the shoe top and bottom together, matching the G symbols and distributing the gathers to fit in the stitching line. Sew the tops to the bottoms by hand with an overcast stitch.
- Punch holes for the laces in the sides of the shoe and make shoe laces of pieces of yarn.
- Make the second shoe in the same way.

MATERIALS
Goldie's Pants
- 14 in × 35 in (.35 m × .9 m) cotton fabric
- 48 in (1.2 m) of ¼ in (.6 cm) elastic

Goldie's Collar
- 31 inches (.8 m) ribbon
- 24 inches (.6 m) lace

Goldie's Shoes
- 8 in × 10 in (.2 m × .25 m) soft leather
- thick cotton yarn to match leather
- strong thread to match leather
- hand-sewing needle
- thimble

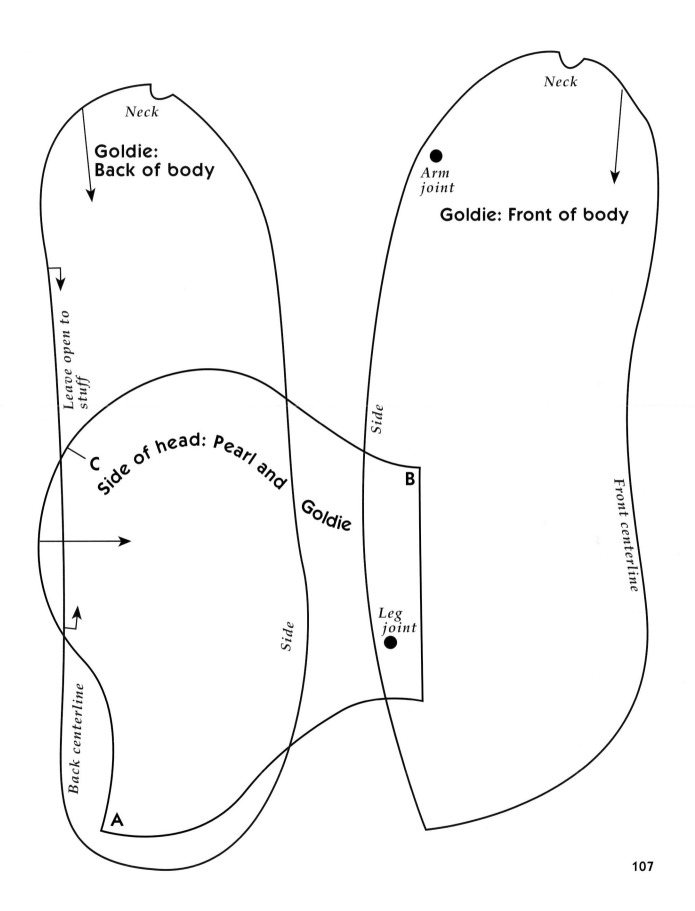

Neck

Goldie: Back of body

Neck

● Arm joint

Goldie: Front of body

Leave open to stuff

C

Side of head: Pearl and Goldie

Side

B

Side

Front centerline

Leg joint

●

Back centerline

A

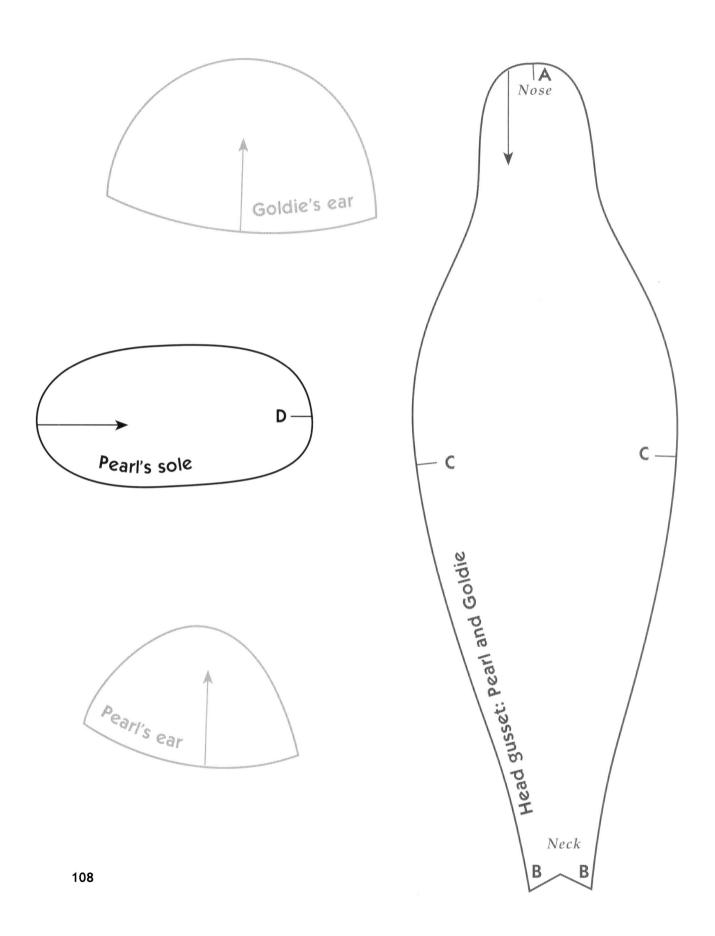

Goldie's ear

Pearl's sole

D

Pearl's ear

A

Nose

C

C

Head gusset: Pearl and Goldie

Neck

B B

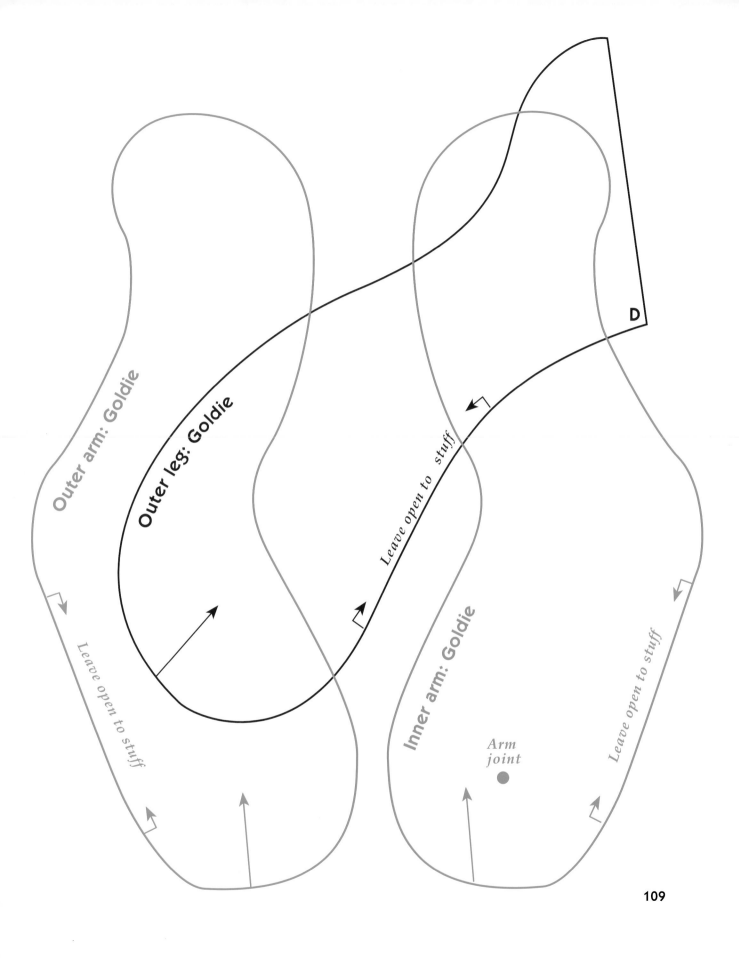

Outer arm: Goldie

Outer leg: Goldie

Leave open to stuff

Leave open to stuff

D

Inner arm: Goldie

Arm joint

Leave open to stuff

Leave open to stuff

109

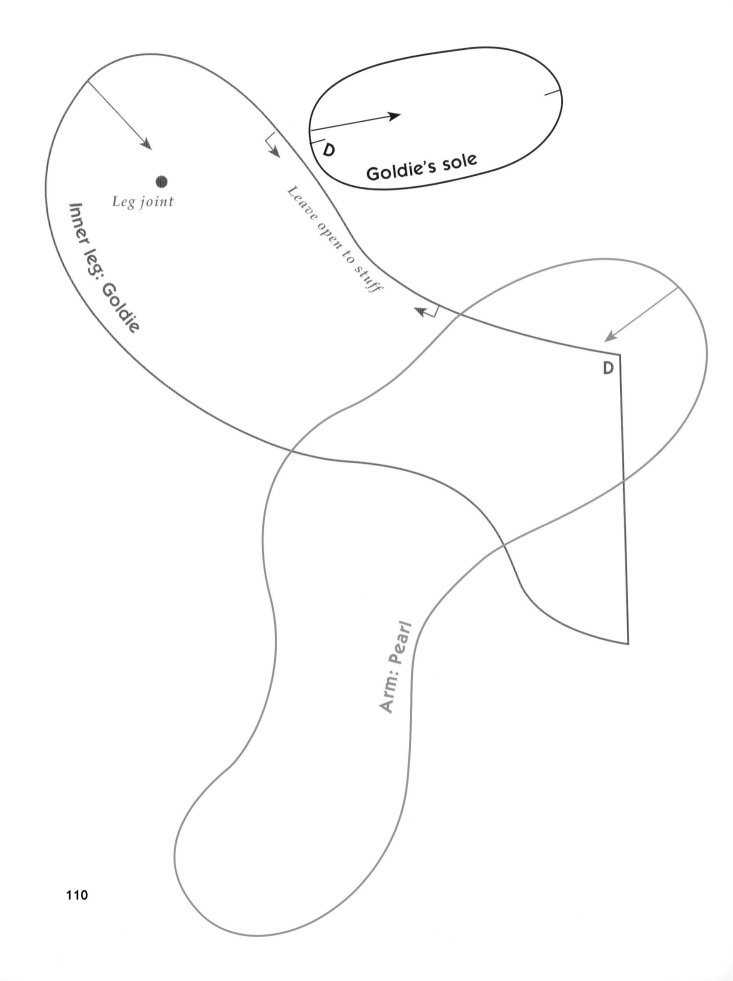

Goldie's sole

Leg joint

Inner leg: Goldie

Leave open to stuff

D

D

Arm: Pearl

110

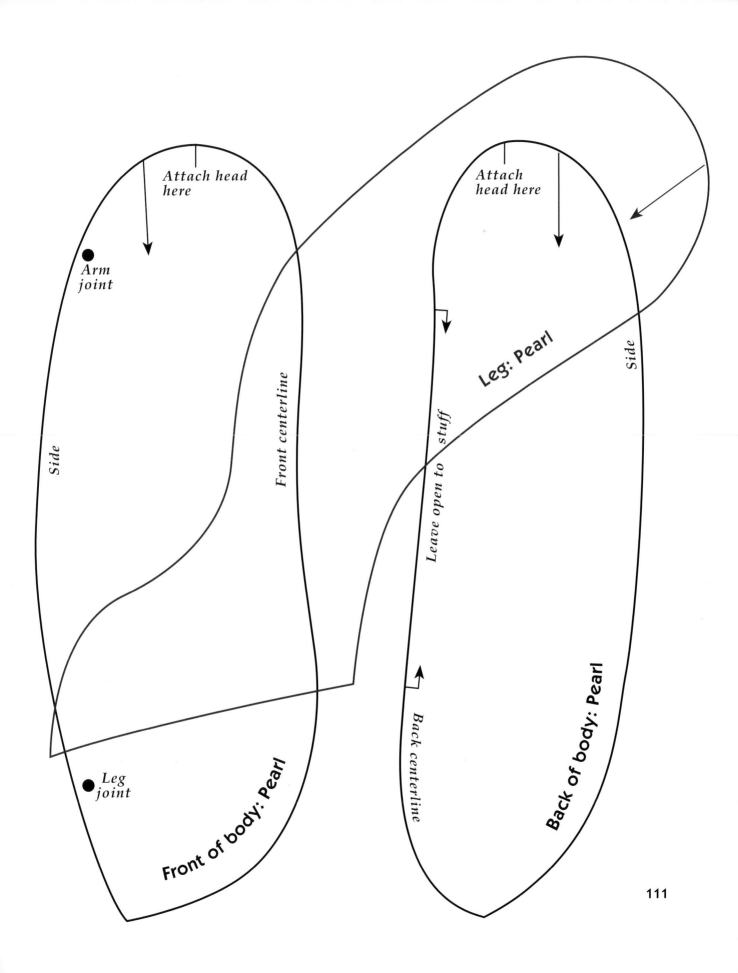

Attach head here

Arm joint

Side

Front centerline

Leg joint

Front of body: Pearl

Attach head here

Leg: Pearl

Side

Leave open to stuff

Back centerline

Back of body: Pearl

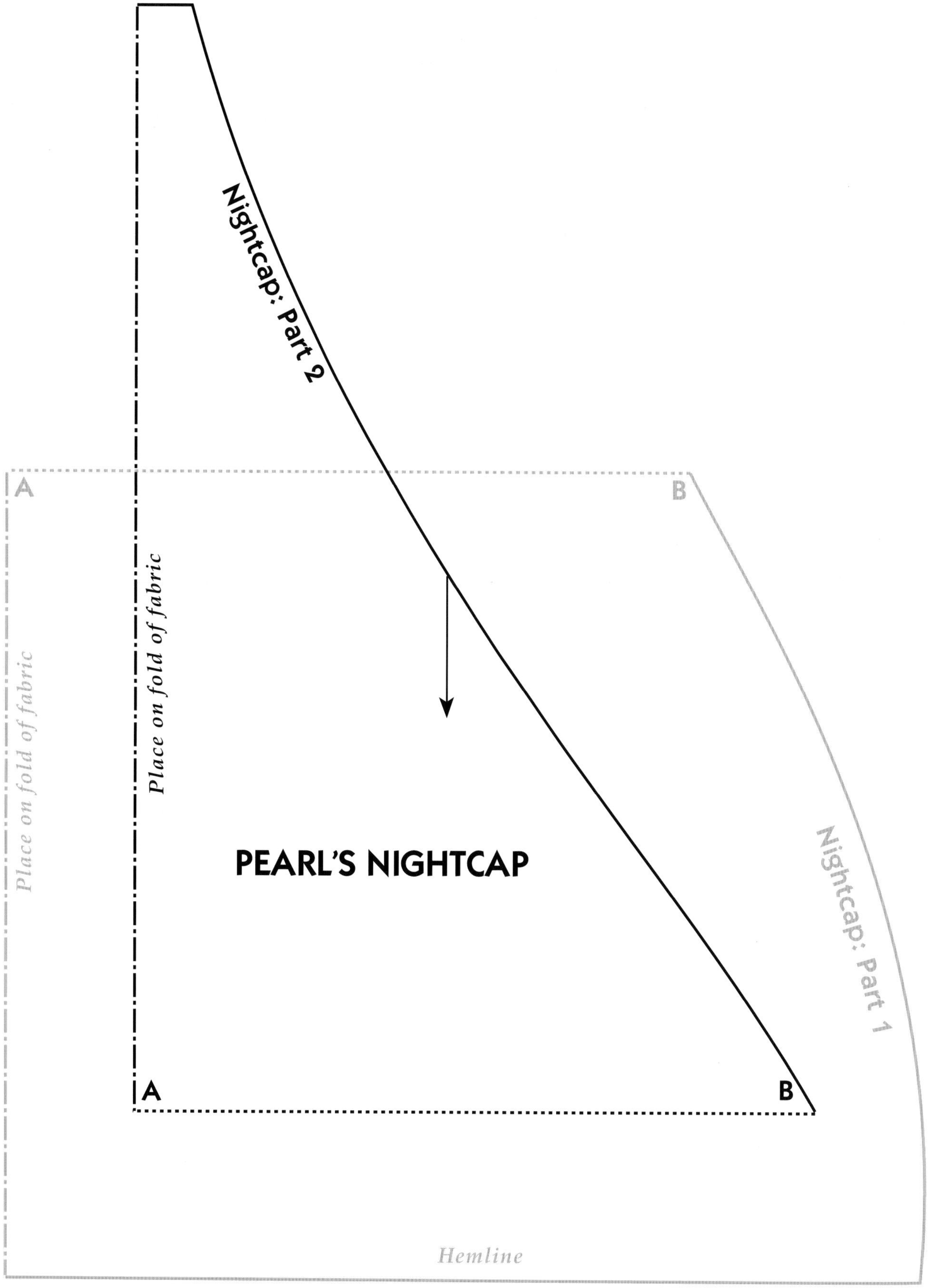

Nightcap: Part 2

Place on fold of fabric

A | | | | | | | | | | | | | | | | | | | | | | | | | | | | | | B

PEARL'S NIGHTCAP

Nightcap: Part 1

A .... B

Hemline

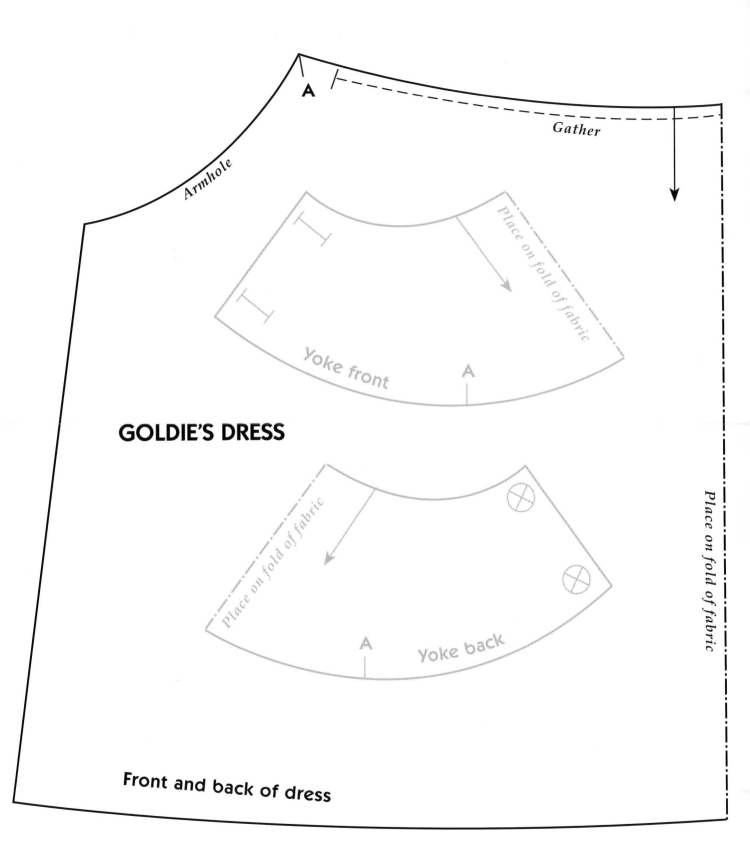

A

Armhole

Gather

Place on fold of fabric

Yoke front

A

GOLDIE'S DRESS

Place on fold of fabric

A

Yoke back

Place on fold of fabric

Front and back of dress

113

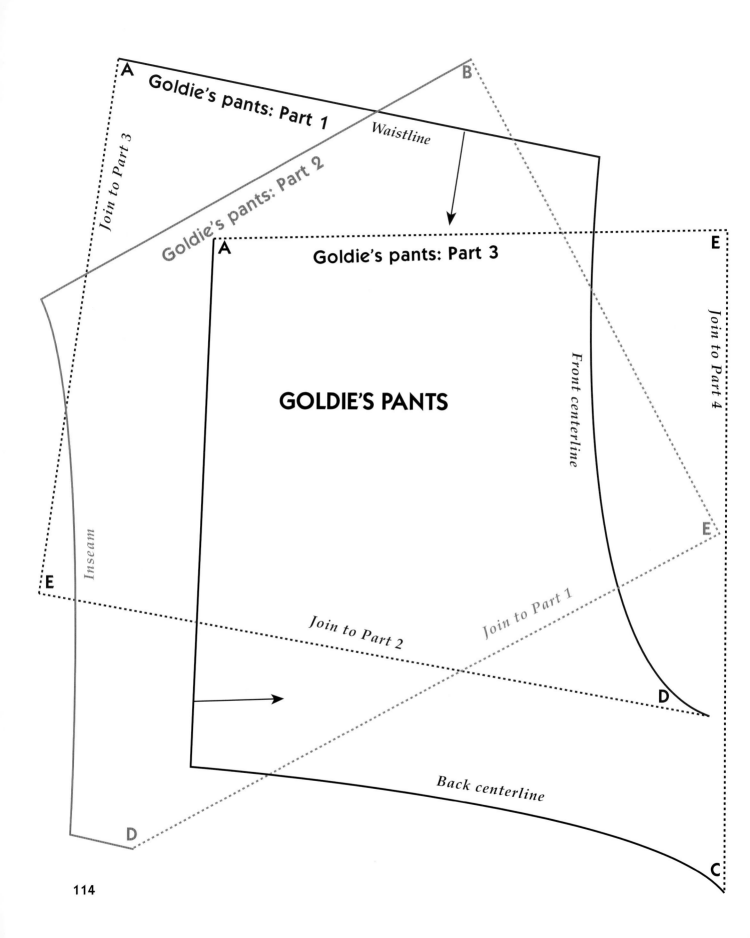

Goldie's pants: Part 1

A

Join to Part 3

Goldie's pants: Part 2

Waistline

A

Goldie's pants: Part 3

B

E

Front centerline

Join to Part 4

E

GOLDIE'S PANTS

Inseam

E

Join to Part 2

Join to Part 1

D

D

Back centerline

C

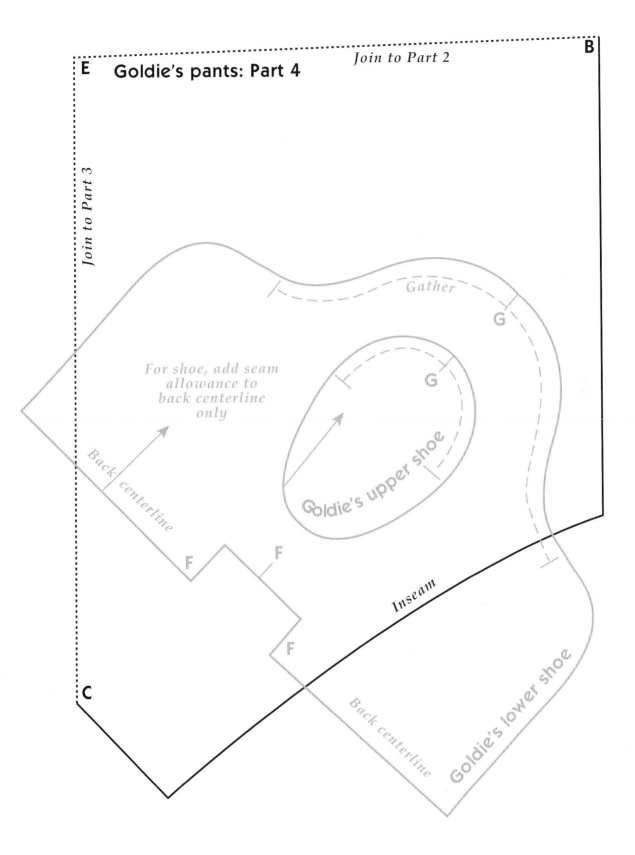

E Goldie's pants: Part 4

Join to Part 2

B

Join to Part 3

Gather

G

For shoe, add seam
allowance to
back centerline
only

G

Goldie's upper shoe

Back centerline

F   F

F

Inseam

C

Back centerline

Goldie's lower shoe

115

HENRIETTA

Henrietta

is 18 inches (45 cm) tall. As her
mouth is open, her pattern is a bit
more complicated than the others.

Reminder: Add seam allowances around the pattern pieces when cutting. Construction is done with right sides of fabric facing, unless noted.

The Bear

Henrietta: Pieces to Cut

Front side of head: cut 2 (1 R)
Back of head: cut 2 (1 R)
Head gusset: cut 1
Front of body: cut 2 (1 R)
Back of body: cut 2 (1 R)
Ear: cut 4 (2 R)
Muzzle part 1: cut 1
Muzzle part 2: cut 1
Muzzle part 3: cut 1 from velvet
Outer arm: cut 2 (1 R)
Inner arm: cut 2 (1 R)
Paw: cut 2 (1 R)
Outer leg: cut 2 (1 R)
Inner leg: cut 2 (1 R)
Sole: cut 2 (1 R)

Sewing Instructions for Bear

- Stitch both front side pieces of the head to the head gusset from A to N (one on each side).
- Stitch the chin seam from F to Q on the two front side of head pieces.
- Stitch the back of head pieces together along the back centerline.
- Stitch together an ear piece and its reverse along the rounded edge;

turn it right-side out, and baste the opening closed, without turning the seam allowance in. Make the second ear the same way.
- Baste each ear to the front of the head from C to P.
- Stitch closed the dart of muzzle piece 1 from O to D.
- Stitch muzzle piece 3 and muzzle piece 1 together along G–D–G.
- Stitch muzzle piece 2 and muzzle piece 3 together along G–E–G.
- Stitch the muzzle to the front side of the head (B–G–F).
- Place the front and back pieces of the head together and stitch the side seams.
- Turn the head right-side out and stuff the head, shaping the mouth in the process.
- Follow the basic techniques chapter to finish Henrietta.

Henrietta's Skirt

- Take the 8 in × 54 in (.2 m × 1.4 m) piece of cotton fabric and stitch the short ends together.
- For the waistband, fold 1¼ inches (3 cm) of the fabric in at one edge of the fabric and pin.
- Along the folded part, stitch two rows of stitches parallel to the edge—one .6 inch (1.5 cm) from the edge and one 1 inch (2.5 cm) from the edge—to make an elastic casing; leave a small opening; insert the elastic.
- Hem the lower edge.

Henrietta's Headband

Fold the long thin piece of cotton fabric in half the long way; stitch the edges closed, leaving an opening to turn right-side out. Stitch the opening closed by hand after turning.

MATERIALS

For the Bear

- 14 in × 54 in (.35 m × 1.4 m) brown woven mohair fur fabric
- 8 in × 8 in (.2 m × .2 m) velvet for paws, soles, and mouth
- pair of black glass eyes, 14 mm size
- joint set for a 22 in tall (55 cm) bear
- 22 oz (600 g) stuffing
- sewing thread to match fur
- black wool yarn for nose and mouth
- strong thread
- growler

For the Clothing

- 8 in × 54 in (.2 m × 1.4 m) cotton fabric for skirt
- 20 in (50 cm) of ¼ in (.6 cm) waistband elastic
- 4 in × 31 in (.1 m × .8 m) cotton fabric for the headband

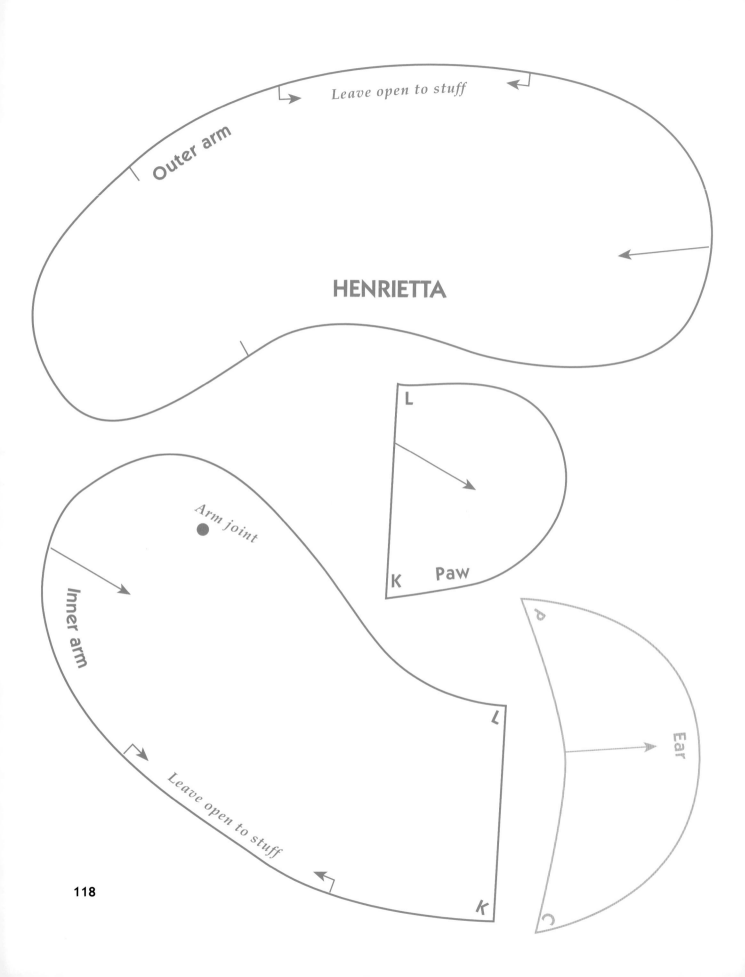

Outer arm

Leave open to stuff

HENRIETTA

L

Arm joint

K   Paw

Inner arm

Leave open to stuff

L

P

Ear

K

C

118

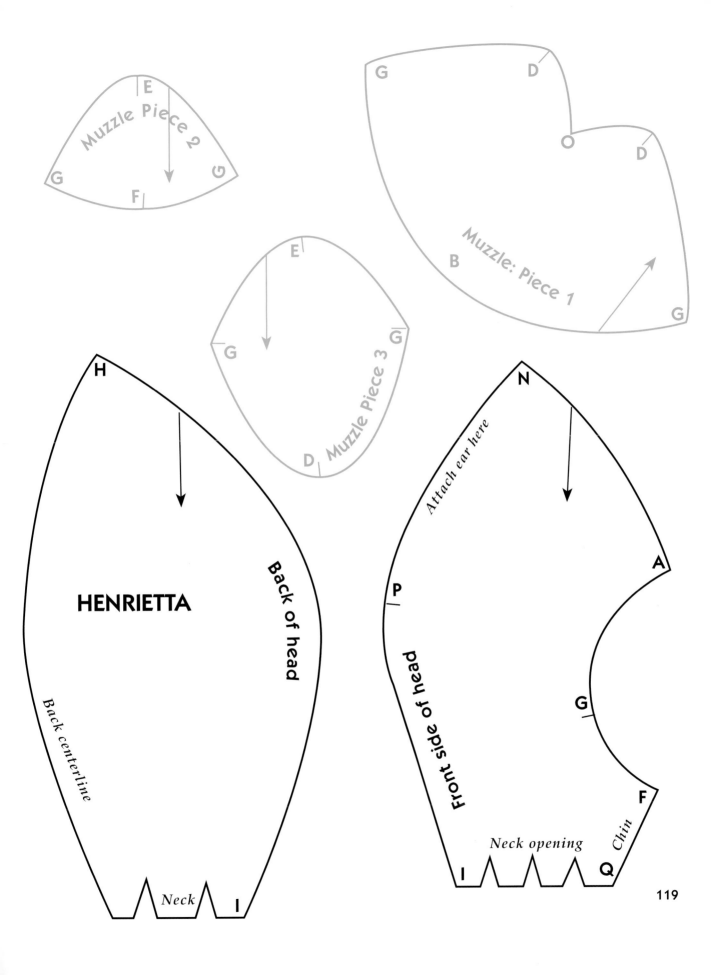

Muzzle Piece 2

E

G   G

F

G   D

O

D

Muzzle: Piece 1

B

G

Muzzle Piece 3

E

G   G

D

H

HENRIETTA

Back of head

Back centerline

Neck

I

N

Attach ear here

A

P

Front side of head

G

F

Chin

Neck opening

I   Q

119

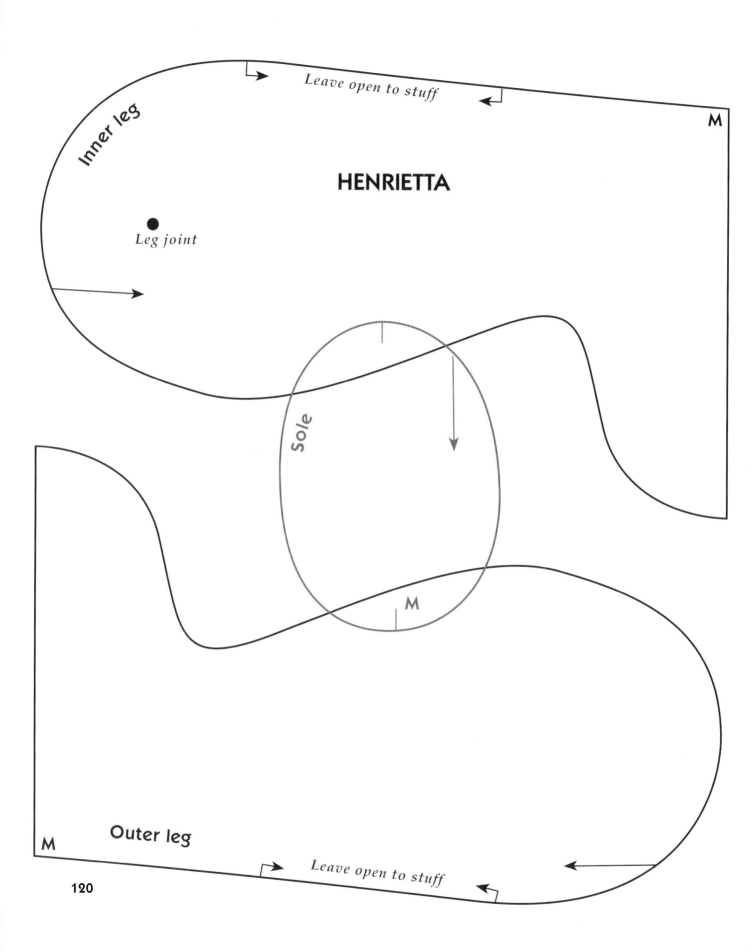

Inner leg

Leg joint

HENRIETTA

Leave open to stuff

M

Sole

M

Outer leg

M

Leave open to stuff

120

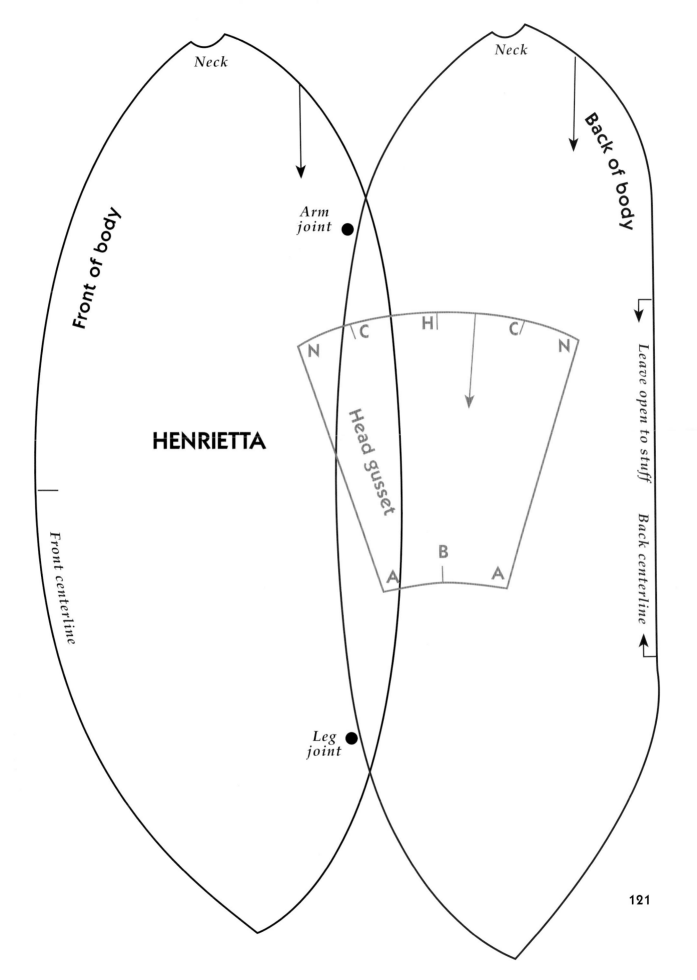

Neck

Neck

Back of body

Front of body

Arm joint ●

HENRIETTA

H

C

N

C

N

Head gusset

Leave open to stuff

Front centerline

B

A

A

Back centerline

Leg joint ●

121

SCOTTY

Scotty

is 12½ inches tall (32 cm). His paws and soles are made from white velvet. He also looks handsome with cotton flannel fabric for soles and paws.*

Reminder: Add seam allowances around the pattern pieces when cutting. Construction is done with right sides of fabric facing, unless noted.

The Bear

Scotty: Pieces to Cut
Side of head: cut 2 (1 R)
Head gusset: cut 1
Arm: cut 2 (1 R)
Paw: cut 2 (1 R)
Ears: cut 4 (2 R)
Front of body: cut 2 (1 R)
Back of body: cut 2 (1 R)
Inner leg: cut 2 (1 R)
Outer leg: cut 2 (1 R)
Sole: cut 2

Sewing Instructions for Bear
Refer to the basic techniques chapter to make Scotty, except for the arms, which are explained below:

• Staystitch outer edges of paws with zigzag stitches; baste them to the arm pieces from F to G, matching letters. Machine-stitch paws to arms ⅛ inch (.3 cm) in from paw edge.

• Make a small cut in the seam allowance at F. Fold the arm in half with right sides facing, pin, and stitch all around, leaving a small opening for stuffing (see page 21 for further details).

Scotty's Overalls

Before you cut fabric: Join sleeve and overalls front patterns from E to F.

Overalls Pieces to Cut
Overalls front: cut 2 (1 R)
Overalls back: cut 2 (1 R)
Pocket: cut 1

Sewing the Overalls
• Hem upper edge of the pocket, fold in the rest of the pocket seam allowances, and stitch the pocket to the right front overalls piece on the outside.

• On the overalls front, fold the facing over to the right side of the fabric and stitch close to the edges from G to I and at the neck edge from the foldline to H along the stitching line.

• Turn the facing inside and iron.

• Stitch overalls back pieces together along back centerline (but not the leg inseam).

• Stitch overalls front pieces together at the front inseam (but not the leg inseam).

• Stitch overalls front and back together at shoulders from A to B.

• Hem the sleeves. Stitch the sleeve underseams and the side seam of the overalls from C to D in one continuous seam for each side.

• Stitch the leg inseams of the overalls front to the leg inseams of the overalls back. Hem the pants legs.

• Finish neck with bias binding. Make buttonholes and sew buttons on overalls front parts. Press lapels.

• Give Scotty a bowtie if you wish.

MATERIALS

For the Bear

- 8 in × 54 in (.2 × 1.4 m) curly white mohair fur fabric
- 6 in × 6 in (.15 × .15 m) white velvet for paws and soles
- pair of brown glass eyes, 8 mm size
- joint set for a 14 inch tall (35 cm) bear
- 18 oz (500 g) stuffing
- sewing thread to match fur
- black embroidery thread
- strong thread

For Overalls

- 10 in × 39 in (.25 × 1 m) plaid flannel
- button
- bias binding
- sewing thread

*If you use flannel, reinforce the paws and soles with interfacing.

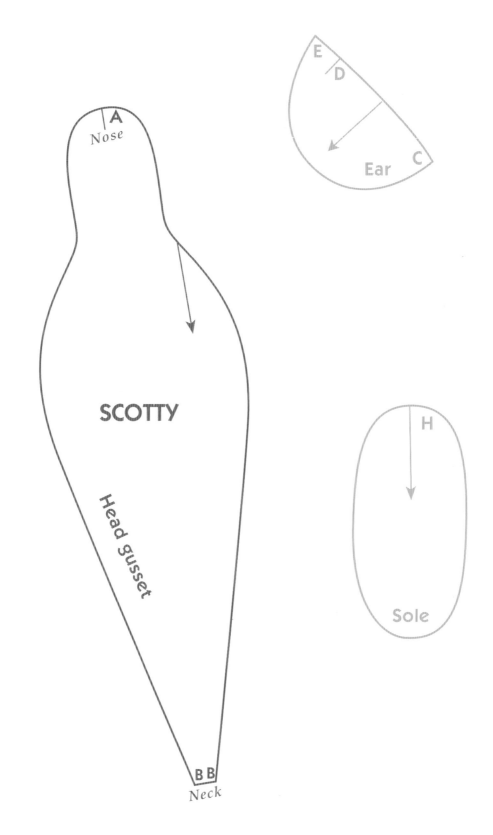

A

Nose

E

D

Ear

C

SCOTTY

Head Gusset

H

Sole

B B

Neck

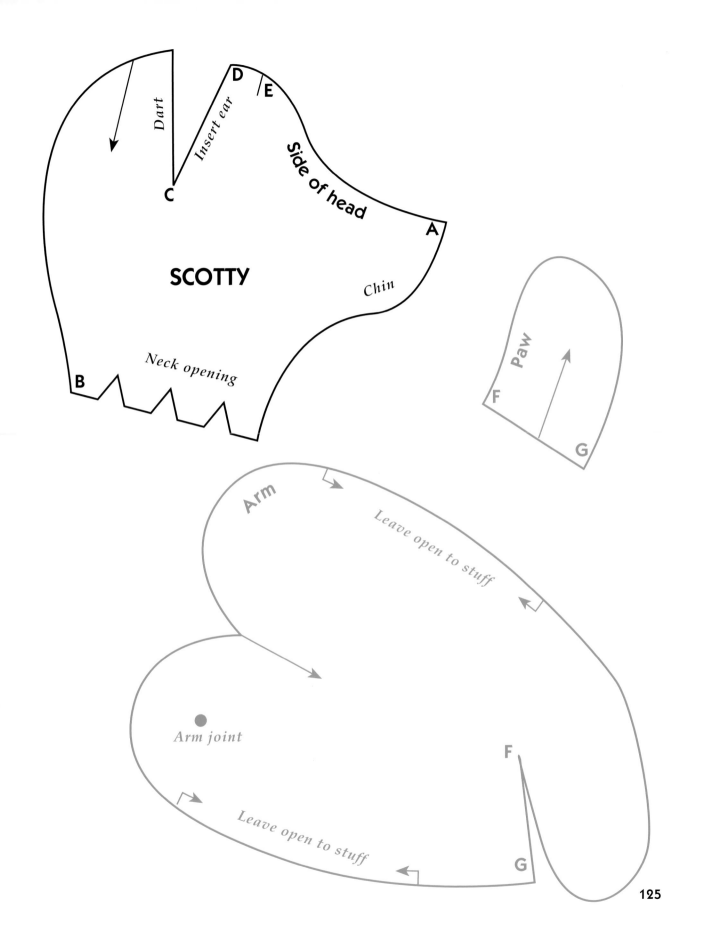

Dart

Insert ear

D E

Side of head

C

A

SCOTTY

Chin

Neck opening

B

Paw

F

G

Arm

Leave open to stuff

Arm joint

Leave open to stuff

F

G

125

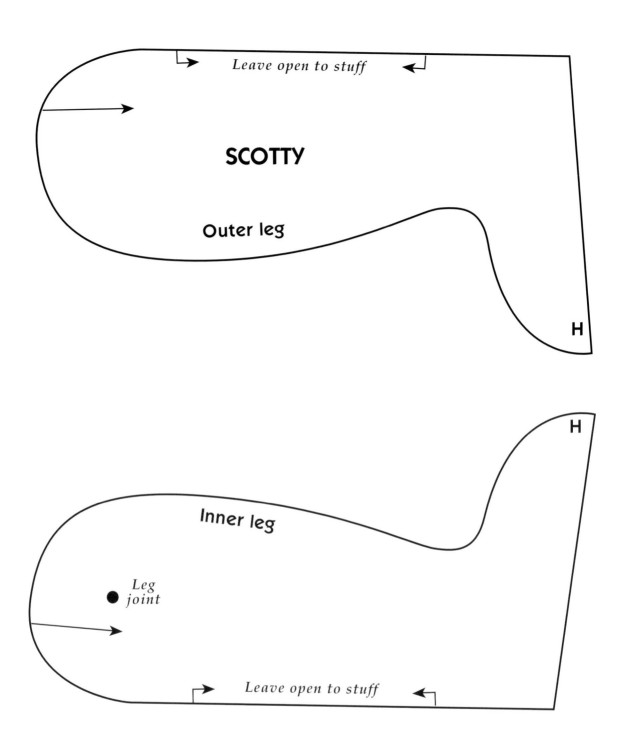

SCOTTY

Outer leg

Inner leg

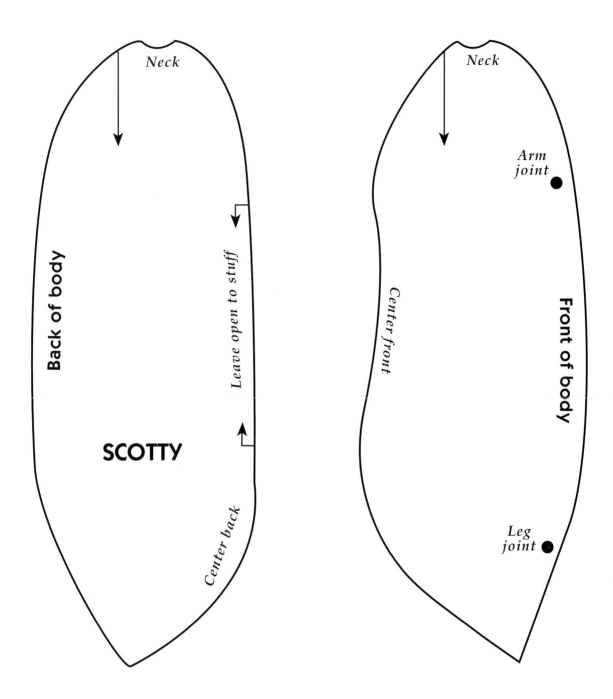

Neck

Back of body

Leave open to stuff

SCOTTY

Center back

Neck

Arm joint

Center front

Front of body

Leg joint

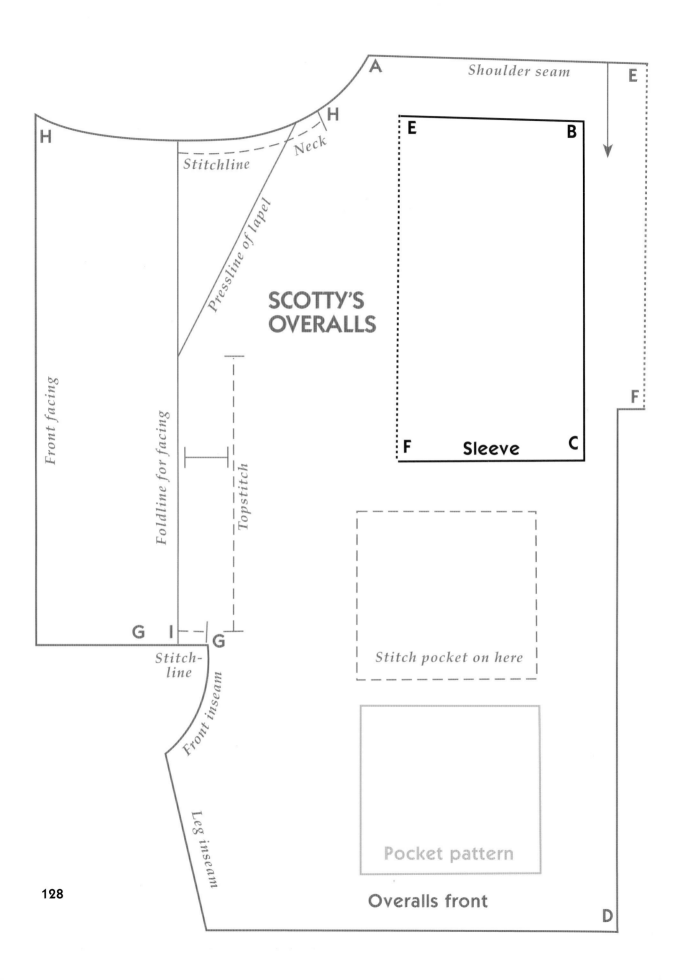

A

Shoulder seam

E

H

H

Neck

Stitchline

E

B

Pressline of lapel

SCOTTY'S
OVERALLS

F

F

Front facing

Foldline for facing

Topstitch

F

Sleeve

C

G I G

Stitch-
line

Front inseam

Stitch pocket on here

Leg inseam

128

Pocket pattern

Overalls front

D

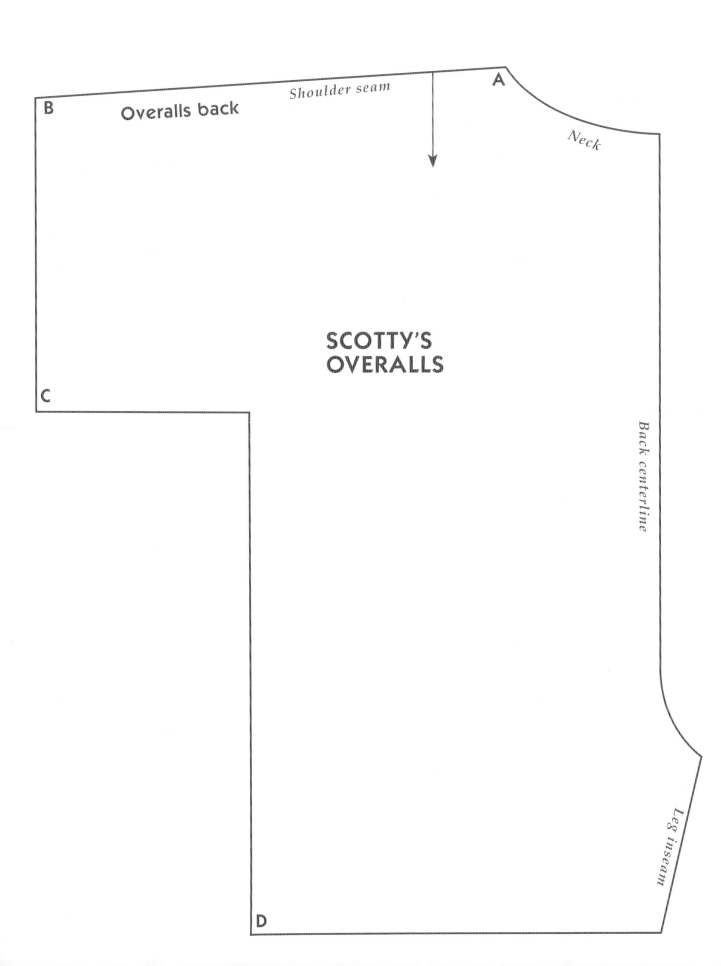

LISA

Lisa

is 10 inches tall (25 cm). This little lady looks best when made with a short-hair mohair plush or even a cotton plush. Her paws and soles may be made from a contrasting material.

Reminder: Add seam allowances around the pattern pieces when cutting. Construction is done with right sides of fabric facing, unless noted.

The Bear

Lisa: Pieces to Cut
Side of head: cut 2 (1 R)
Head gusset: cut 1
Ear: cut 4 (2 R)
Front of body: cut 2 (1 R)
Back of body: cut 2 (1 R)
Outer arm: cut 2 (1 R)
Inner arm: cut 2 (1 R)
Paw: cut 2 (1 R)
Inner leg: cut 2 (1 R)
Outer leg: cut 4 (2 R)
Sole: cut 2

Sewing Instructions for Bear
Follow the basic techniques chapter to make Lisa.

Lisa's Dress

Dress Pieces to Cut
Dress front: cut 1 on folded fabric
Dress back: cut 2 (1 R)
Sleeve: cut 2 (1 R)

Yoke front: cut 1
Yoke back: cut 2 (1 R)

Sewing the Dress
- Stitch the back yoke pieces to the front yoke from G to H. Set aside.
- Stitch the sleeves to the front and dress from A to B and C to D.
- Run two rows of basting stitches around the upper edge of the dress to gather, starting at the center back. Pull the basting so the top of the dress fits with the lower edge of the yoke. Match the letters D on yoke to D's on the dress, and distribute the gathers evenly. Pin the dress to the yoke and sew it on.
- Hem sleeves to make a casing for elastic. Insert elastic; adjust the elastic length to fit bear's arms. Keep elastic ends in place with pins.
- Stitch the seams of the sleeves and dress as one seam on both sides from the sleeve edge to A; pivot at C and sew down to F (lower edge). The elastic ends are sewn into the seam at the same time.
- Neaten up the lower edge of the dress if necessary. Sew lace on the right side of the bottom of the dress with raw edges aligned; fold and turn under the hem and raw edge of lace, and stitch in place.
- Stitch the back seam closed up to K. Fold seam allowances inside. Machine stitch around the opening from K to J close to the edge.
- Gather the lace to fit the neckline and baste in place. Finish with bias binding around the neckline.
- Sew on snaps to close the back.
- **Optional:** Use thin yarn to crochet a pocketbook; give Lisa a bow made from the same fabric you used to make the dress.

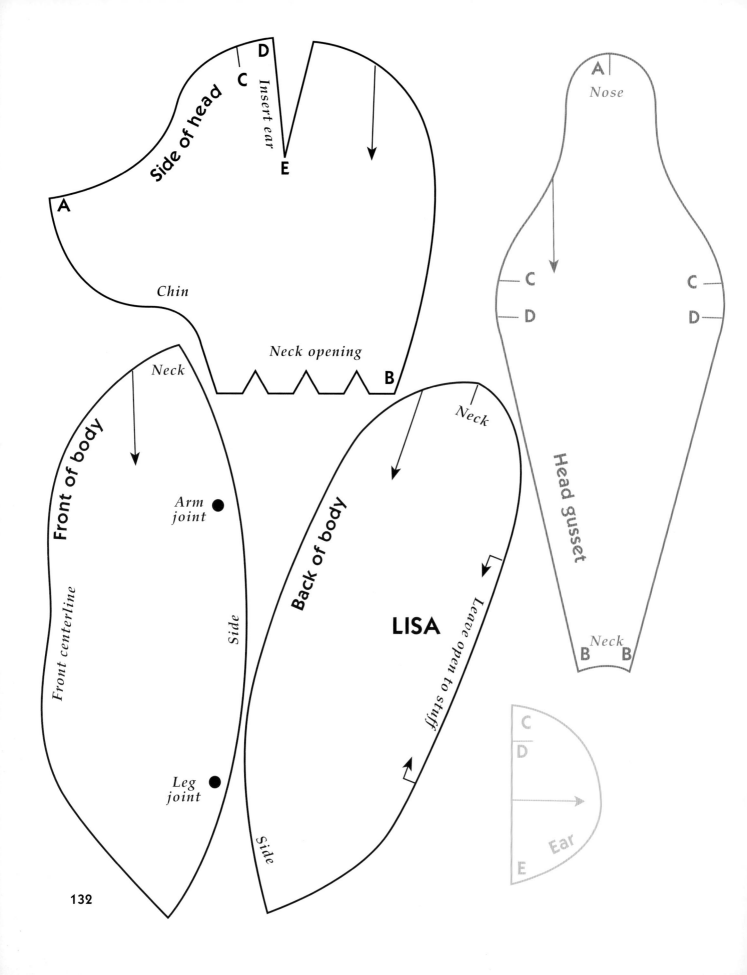

Side of head

D

C

Insert ear

E

A

Chin

Neck opening

B

Neck

Front of body

Front centerline

Arm joint ●

Side

Leg joint ●

Back of body

Neck

LISA

Leave open to stuff

Side

A

Nose

C   C

D   D

Head gusset

B *Neck* B

C

D

Ear

E

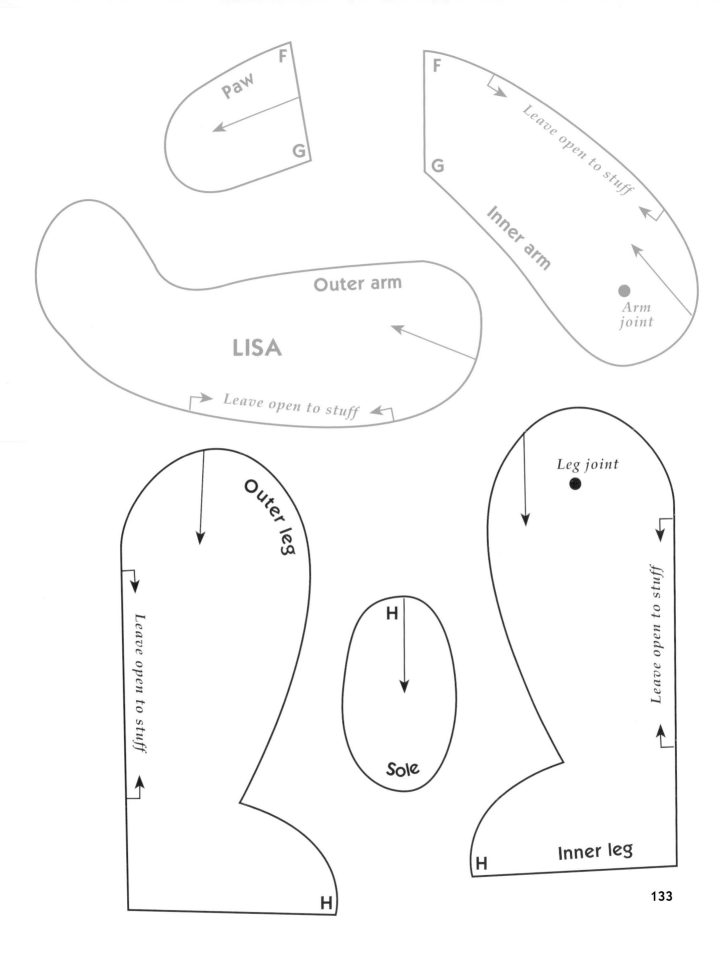

Paw

F

G

F

Leave open to stuff

G

Inner arm

Arm joint

Outer arm

LISA

Leave open to stuff

Outer leg

Leave open to stuff

Leg joint

Leave open to stuff

H

Sole

H

Inner leg

H

133

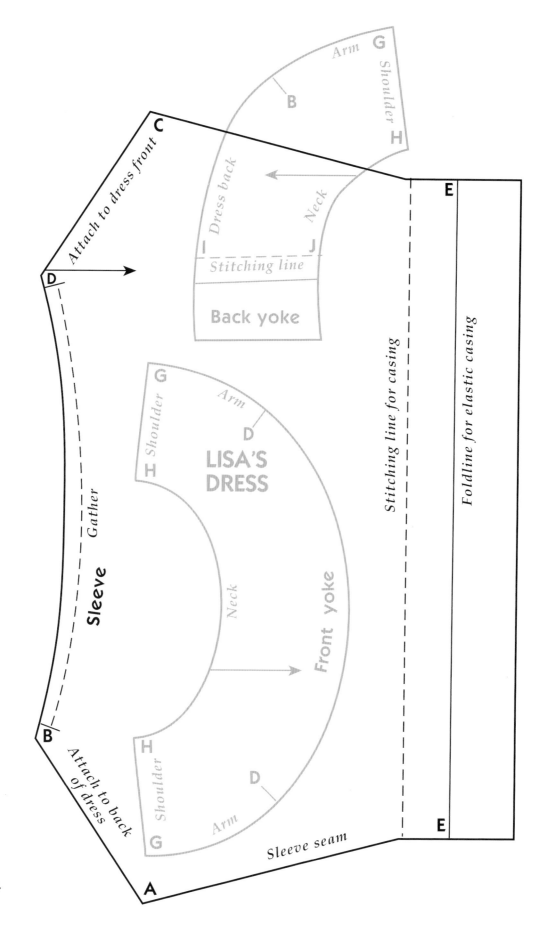

C

Attach to dress front

D

Sleeve

Gather

B

Attach to back
of dress

A

134

Arm G

B

Shoulder

H

Dress back

Neck

I   J

Stitching line

Back yoke

G

Shoulder

Arm

D

H

**LISA'S
DRESS**

Neck

Front yoke

H

Shoulder

D

Arm

G

Sleeve seam

E

Stitching line for casing

Foldline for elastic casing

E

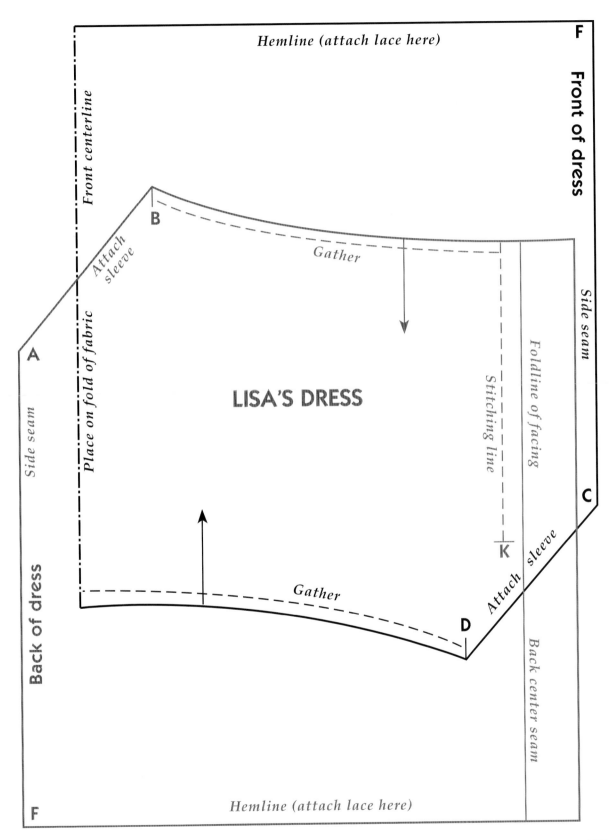

Front of dress

Hemline (attach lace here)

F

Front centerline

B

Attach sleeve

Gather

Place on fold of fabric

A

Side seam

LISA'S DRESS

Side seam

C

Stitching line

Foldline of facing

K

Attach sleeve

Back of dress

Gather

D

Back center seam

F

Hemline (attach lace here)

BROWNIE

◆ *Brownie*

is 19½ inches tall (50 cm) and has a jointed head. Make him with white plush and you change the brown bear to a polar bear. If you do this, do not shave the fur around his nose.

Reminder: Add seam allowances around the pattern pieces when cutting. Construction is done with right sides of fabric facing, unless noted.

Before you cut fabric: To fit in this book, we divided the side of body pattern into 4 parts and the underbody pattern into 2 parts. Join the paper pattern parts after tracing:

• Join underbody patterns part 1 and part 2 along line E–F to make the whole underbody pattern.
• Join side of body parts 1 and 2 along line A–B.
• Join side of body parts 3 and 4 along line B–H.
• Join the combined side of body parts 1+2 and 3+4 along line C–B–D to make the whole side of body pattern.

Brownie: Pieces to Cut

Side of head: cut 2 (1 R)
Head gusset: cut 1
Ear: cut 4 (2 R)
Chin gusset: cut 1
Side of body: cut 2 (1 R)
Underbody: cut 2 (1 R)
Tail: cut 1
Sole: cut 4

Sewing Instructions for Bear

• Stitch together the two underbody parts from I to J, leaving an opening for stuffing.
• Pin and stitch the underbody to each side of body piece from J down to K, across from K to L, around the curve from L to M, across to N, and up the rump to I.
• Fold the tail piece in half and stitch it to itself on the rounded side. Turn it right-side out and baste it to the body above I, with raw edges aligned, tail facing in. (The body is still inside out.)
• Stitch the side of body pieces together along the top center seam, all the way from I (below the tail) to the neck joint., leaving a small opening to insert the neck joint.
• Sew the soles in place on the feet.
• To make the head, pin and stitch each side of head to the head gusset from O to Q. Stitch the two sides of the head to each other from O to R. Pin and stitch the chin gusset to each side of the head from R to T.
• Stuff, finish, and attach the head following instructions in basic techniques chapter. Shave the pile around the bear's upper snout. Embroider nose as shown at right.
• Sew the ears on the stuffed head, curving them slightly.
• Shorten an old belt for a collar.

MATERIALS FOR BEAR

☐ 16 in × 54 in (.4 m × 1.4 m) brown fur
☐ pair of black glass eyes, 20 mm size
☐ head joint for 19½ inch tall (50 cm) bear
☐ 54 oz (1500 g) stuffing
☐ sewing thread to match fur
☐ black pearl embroidery yarn
☐ strong thread

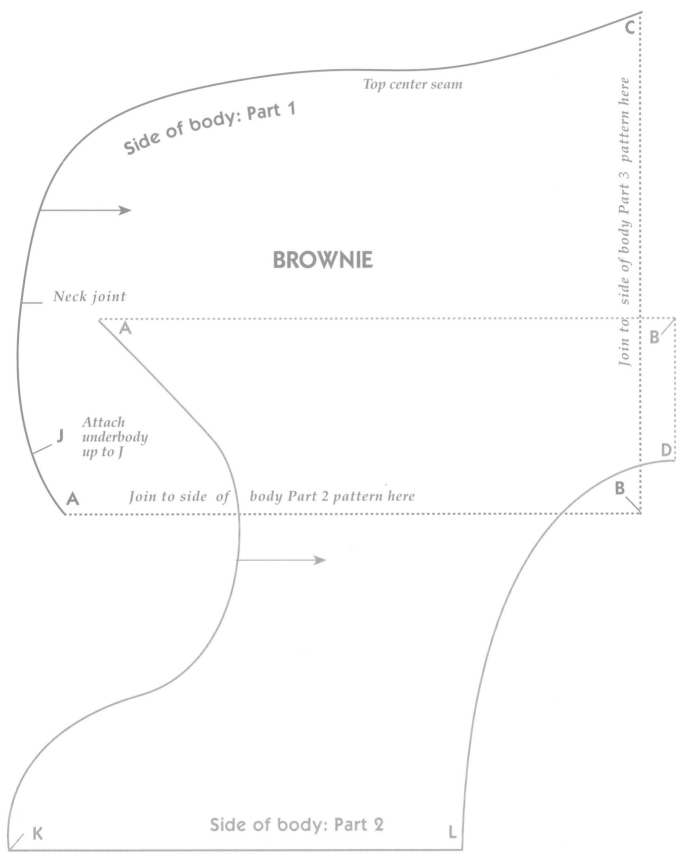

Side of body: Part 1

Top center seam

Join to side of body Part 3 pattern here

BROWNIE

Neck joint

A

B

D

Attach
underbody
up to J

J

A

Join to side of body Part 2 pattern here

B

K

Side of body: Part 2

L

138

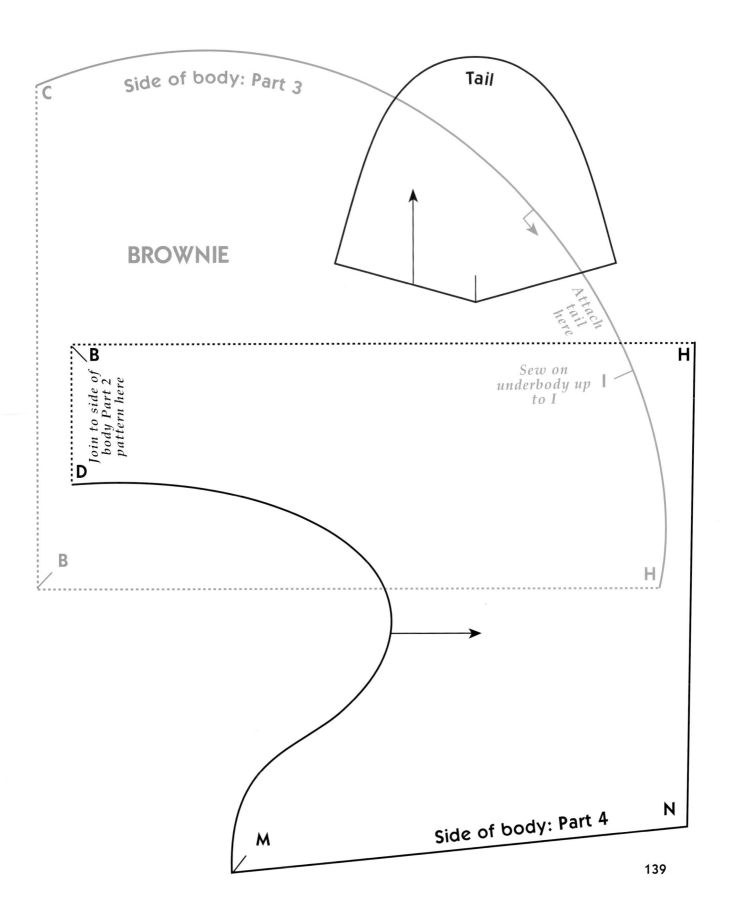

Side of body: Part 3

C

Tail

BROWNIE

Attach tail here

B

H

Join to side of body Part 2 pattern here

Sew on underbody up to I

I

D

B

H

M

N

Side of body: Part 4

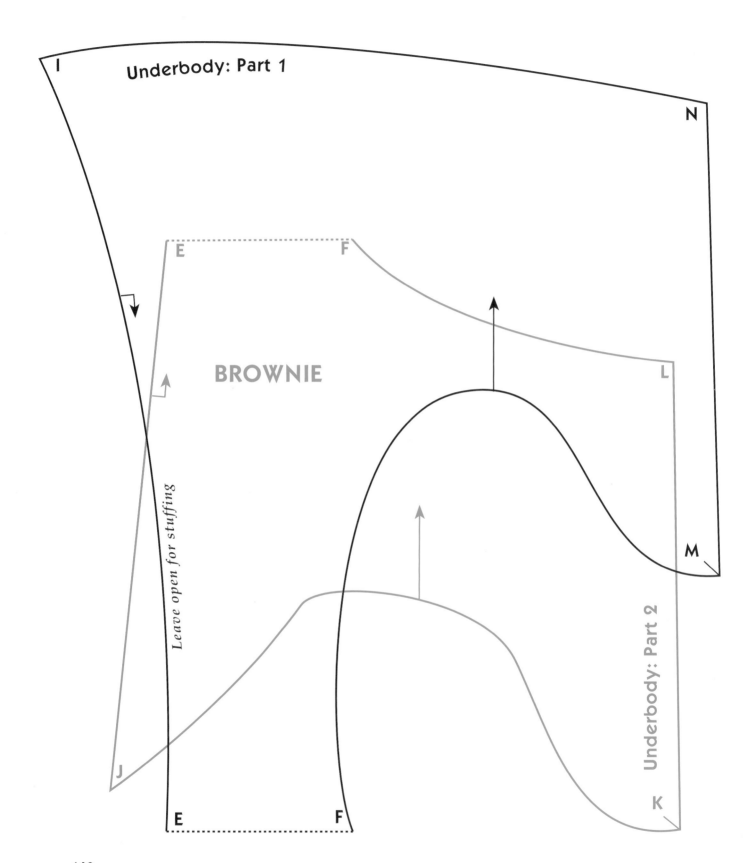

Underbody: Part 1

I

N

E F

BROWNIE

L

M

Leave open for stuffing

Underbody: Part 2

J

E F

K

140

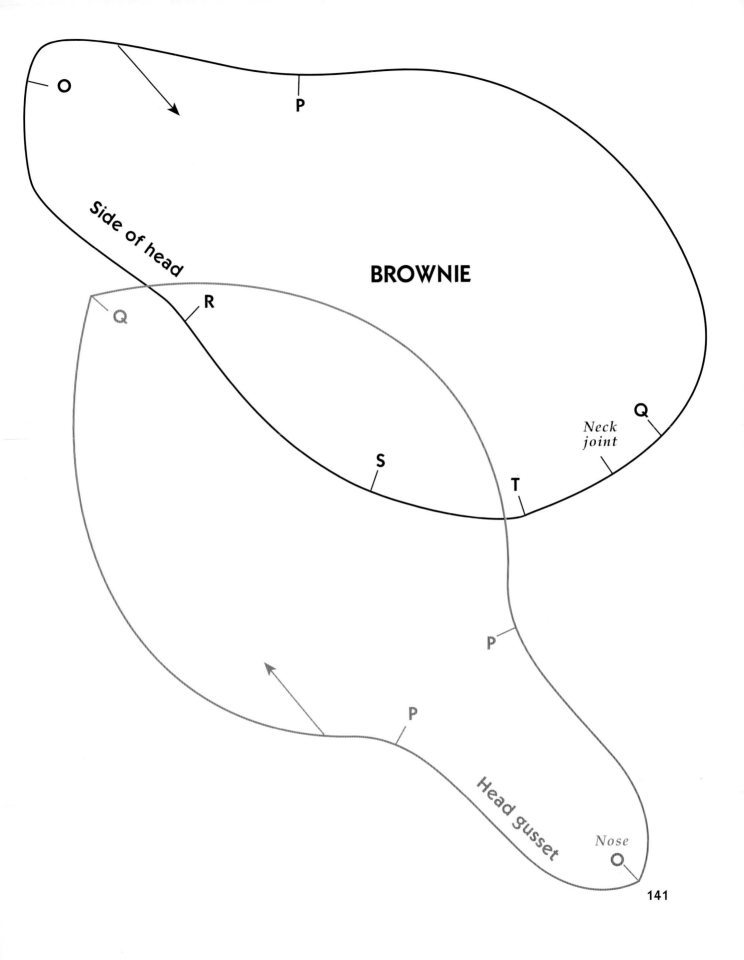

O

P

Side of head

BROWNIE

Q

R

S

T

Neck joint

Q

P

P

Head gusset

Nose

O

141

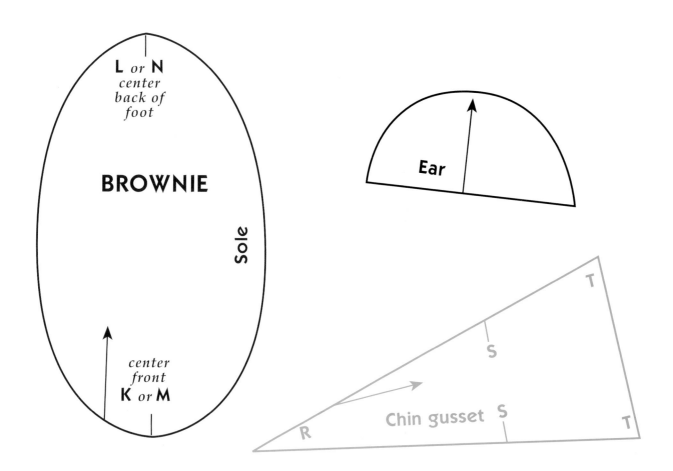

BROWNIE

L or N
center
back of
foot

Sole

center
front
K or M

Ear

T

S

R

Chin gusset   S

T

A WORD FROM THE AUTHORS

Teddy bears have been constant companions for young and old for almost 100 years. Generations of children cuddled and loved them intensely, and threw them into corners in fits of anger, only to pick them up again with feelings of great regret.

Teddy bears know about the joys and agonies of growing up; we share with them our first heartbreak, and let our tears be absorbed in their soft fur. Teddy bears often accompany us when we venture out into the world. They are often relegated to the attic for years, with ears torn and paws worn bare, and then undergo seemingly magical rejuvenation so they can be given to the next generation.

What made us decide to make our own teddy bears? In the beginning, all we wanted was to make teddy bears for our children. While searching for proper materials and patterns, we became afflicted with the "disease" called *arctophily*—a name derived from the Greek *arcto* (bear) and *philos* (love). For weeks and months on end, our living rooms looked like warehouses of fluffy, furry material. Arms, legs, eyes, joints, and fabrics in every size and color "bearly" left room for the men and children to find a comfortable place to sit. But they endured, and did so with great equanimity. Criticism and approval was always welcome.

The result is the book you are holding in your hands, a book in which teddy bear lovers will find a few of the models we developed. It is our hope that you have as much fun creating your teddy bear as we did. But—let us caution you—it is contagious!

INDEX

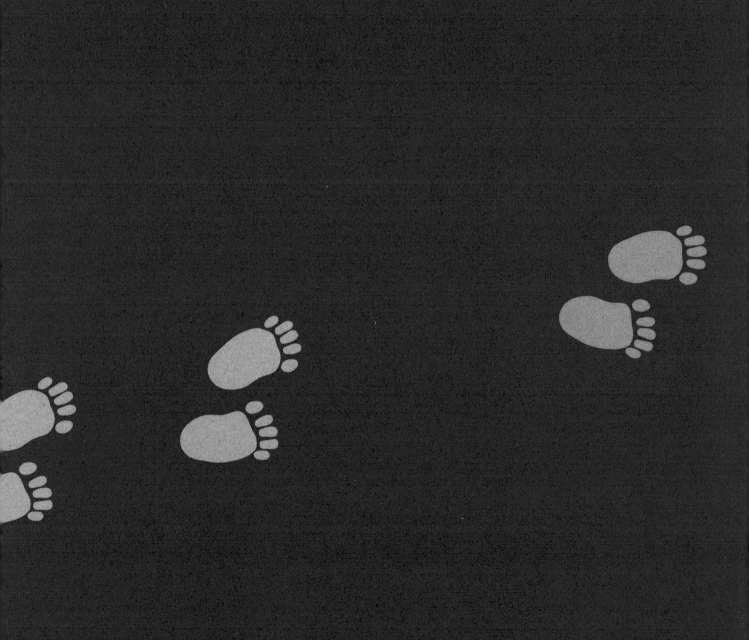